I will never
See, upon th [P9-CEI-375]
my hands I have written
your name.

Isaiah 49: 15-16

This Blessed Mess

Finding
Hope
Amidst
Life's
Chaos

This
Blessed
Mess

"Pat Livingston gives us eyes
for the hidden treasures of our lives."

~Henri J. M. Nouwen

Patricia H. Livingston

SORIN BOOKS   Notre Dame, Indiana

First printing, August, 2000
Second printing, February, 2001
29,000 copies in print

International Standard Book Number: 1-893732-16-9 CB
                                     1-893732-15-0 PB
Library of Congress Card Number: 00-101264
Cover design by Kathy Coleman
Text design by Brian C. Conley
Printed and bound in the United States of America.

Dedication

*Companion: from the Latin "com" meaning "with"
and "pan" meaning "bread";
One with whom I break bread*

To my companions:

  those with whom I have, and do, and will
  break bread
  as we make our way
  in the adventure of living,
  sharing meals of all kinds:
  in cluttered kitchens and elegant restaurants,
  in cafeterias of academe and cars after drive-throughs,
  on airplane tray tables and hospital bedsides,
  and especially around many beloved dining room tables,
  particularly my own, which is the table
  our family gathered around as I grew up;
  and with all of you at the common table of our daily living
  in which we ourselves are broken open
  and poured out again and again.

  I dedicate this book to you,
  through whom I know for certain
  that I am not alone,
  that there will be blessing in the mess,
  and that on the other side of pain,
  and even in the midst of pain,
  there can be laughter.

  It is through you I know best the Companion at the heart
  of Life.

Contents

I n t r o d u c t i o n

This is a book about struggle.

It is about how struggle overtakes us without our permission. It is about what lies within struggle and beyond it. It is about what we can do with struggle and what it can do with us.

Material for this book has been gathering in me for thirty-five years, since I first faced reality as a young adult and strained to comprehend the dynamics of life's difficulty.

I write out of my experience, recognizing clearly that my life has been far less painful than the lives of so many around the world and across time. This book is simply an expression of my effort to understand my own events, shared in the hope that it might speak to the lives of others.

A collection of what is especially meaningful to me is offered here—insights and images from my own life, from study and conversation, from songs and books. Mostly there are stories. All of them point to the same thing: Life is filled with struggle. Struggle is filled with Love.

Life is, as the title says, "This Blessed Mess."

The first half of the book is an attempt to describe how this process reveals itself: "The Interplay of Chaos and Creation."

The rest of the book is about dealing with the challenge, offering practical ways to resist being deadened by the mysterious dance. What helps? How do we hold on long enough to know "it ain't over 'til it's over"? The second half is: "What Helps Us Move to Creation."

These understandings, wrung from my living, have made a difference to me. I offer them in case they might be of some encouragement to you.

As you read, I hope that my stories will remind you of stories of your own; that my insights will confirm your own conclusions; that my activities and prayers will connect with ways, transcendent and pragmatic, you have found for "heartening." Sometime, perhaps, you'll pass yours on to me.

Part One
The Interplay of Chaos and Creation

I

Coming Across Chaos

"What a year we're having," my neighbor commented as we walked toward our cars enveloped in the acrid smell of smoke thick in the mid-morning air. Vast stretches of Florida were burning, and the wind brought a stinging reminder to our eyes. "First tornadoes, then the floods, now the fires. It's like chaos keeps coming."

"Chaos keeps coming" is a fair description of life, and it took me a very long time to really understand that truth. Little in my childhood or education prepared me for how hard life can be. Maybe it was thought that children should be protected, or maybe I just missed the warnings.

For a long time I believed that events unfolded in a certain expectable way, and that, in the lives of people who tried to do what they were supposed to do, there would always be a kind of peace and stability.

One reason I believed this for so long was that we had a very orderly household. Both Mom and Dad were very organized: he as an Army general and she as an English teacher.

I graduated from high school in 1959, having lived more than half my life in the famous Fifties; the *Leave It to Beaver* and *Father Knows Best* years that are used as a metaphor for a secure and predictable period. This decade is sometimes called "The Eisenhower Era," and I not only lived in it, I even began it by attending Eisenhower's inaugural parade!

13

There was actually an event connected with Eisenhower that could have served as a little warning about chaos, if I had taken note of it. Mom and Dad were invited to the White House for an official dinner. Mom had very thin, fine hair, hard to style in any elegant fashion, and she was trying to look her best for the dinner. She had placed a curler in the front of her hair to give it a little lift, and was planning to remove it at the very last minute. Dad's assignment was to remind her.

Apparently, when they pulled up at the White House there was a lot of activity and confusion: doors being opened, Secret Service checks taking place. In any event, when she came home she still had the curler in her hair! "Oh no . . ." we heard her cry out as she glanced in the mirror, "George! You never reminded me!" If I had only known the significance, this event could have provided some droll notice about things not turning out as planned.

Growing up, we lived adhering to schedules. Sheets were changed on every bed each Monday. Mattresses were turned once a month. (One month they were turned side to side, the next month up to down.) Meals were eaten at about the same time every day, and dishes were always done right after the final plates were cleared. There were schedules for when the windows were washed, the shutters repainted, and the closets cleaned. A list was hung on a bulletin board in the kitchen to write down any item that was used up (the mustard, for example) so it could be replaced at the next trip to the store.

That order provided me with a great sense of security in those formative years. The world-view taken for granted was: "if you behave yourself, if you conscientiously do the things you are taught, somehow all will be well."

The same view was reinforced in school. The private academy I attended was a superb place for learning, the most orderly of all environments. There were medals, cards, and ribbons given out at a weekly assembly of the student body to those who were not only good students, but also to those who were seen as especially cooperative, polite, and neat. We even wore white gloves with our uniforms to this ceremony.

Thriving in this atmosphere, I set new school records for cooperation. My senior year I was what they called the "Head Blue Ribbon."

I can still see our small class of young women at graduation dressed in laced-trimmed, white organdy dresses for the ceremony on the front lawn. Dark green laurel wreaths were on our heads, our faces filled with innocence and wonder, idealism and eager hope.

College followed graduation, then I married very young, to a newly graduated West Point officer. Soon thereafter things stopped proceeding in an orderly fashion. Chaos began creeping in.

As a new Army couple we endured the upheaval of moving about once a year. Things were just about unpacked in one place when it was time to think about repacking them again. Babies were born one after the other, all of them born weeks overdue, none of them sleeping through the night until they were at least two *years* old.

Laundry seemed to breed and multiply in the hamper until the only space not filled with clothes to be washed was filled with dishes to be done or toys to be put away.

I loved the children totally: Kadee, Randy, and Boo (known to his adult colleagues as Rob, Boo's real name is Robert). But in the middle of my loving them, I was often overwhelmed by the unpredictability of motherhood. The sudden high fevers, the incredible pranks, the accidents shattered my calm. Boo fell out of a shopping cart and broke his arm. Randy ran through the sliding glass door and had hundreds of stitches. Kadee got the worst case of chickenpox the pediatrician had ever seen, with pox even in the whites of her eyes. All three were up for any adventure, and what one didn't think of, the others did. Sometimes babysitters made elaborate excuses not to return.

Little by little I was forced to let go of my notion of an orderly universe. At least any life *I* was able to manage was not tranquil and on schedule. What was expected often did not happen; what was dreaded often did. Most unimaginable of all, after thirteen years, there was a divorce.

If anyone had told me, standing on the long green lawn of the academy, in my white organdy graduation dress with my blue ribbon and laurel wreath, that I would be divorced from the father of my children, I would have simply said: "You are totally mistaken."

In the disorder of divorce I felt overcome by chaos. "And where is God in all of this?" I anguished. It was a very big question.

In the years that led up to the divorce and in the subsequent years, off and on, in many varied circumstances, I have been wrestling with the question of finding God in chaos. Now I realize that this is a familiar human challenge—the times of disappointment and disillusion, fear and failure, illness and anxiety, and the confusion of where God might be in the unfolding of it all.

I know that what I have been asked to endure is very little compared with the magnitude of suffering in so many lives. That I was sheltered for so long was a rare privilege, and gave me an artificial view of reality. What I hope to point out is that, however our lives unfold, there is a common drama of the human condition. Each of us is overtaken by storms of difficulty as we make our way. No one remains untouched by chaos.

2

The Science
of Chaos

*Clouds are not spheres. Mountains are not cones.
Lightning does not travel in a straight line.*

—James Gleick

Trying to come to grips with the havoc of chaos in my life, I
have been both fascinated and somehow deeply comforted to
discover that there is a chaos theory in physics and mathematics. I have added it to other treasured insights that have helped
me in my trying to understand upheaval.

Chaos theory has been formulated after great struggle by
scientists in the second half of this century. Their story reminds
me of my own. The stages of the evolving of their theory are
similar to the stages I have gone through trying to make some
sense of my life.

The first scientific stage, paralleling my first stage, was the
experience of an orderly world. Hidden in what was considered objective experience was the unquestioned assumption
that order is permanent and universal.

The world of Newtonian physics and Euclidian geometry,
where natural laws governed all, was like the world of our family in the Eisenhower era where you always had a clean linen
handkerchief and had nametags neatly sewn in all your school

clothes. It was an era of simple, certain answers to familiar questions. "Where is God in chaos?" was not one of them.

The second stage for the scientists and for me was the stage where the assumption that life is orderly was challenged by the undeniable reality of chaos.

In James Gleick's absorbing bestseller, *Chaos: Making a New Science*, he describes how scientists using modern technology came upon happenings that did not fit the theories and equations of classic science.

Amazingly, for centuries, when scientists found discrepancies that did not fit the theories, they were discarded as errors and ignored. The researchers just assumed there had been some mistake, or that the numbers studied were too small to be taken into consideration.

With the accuracy available in modern computers, however, it became much harder to dismiss what did not fit. Beginning in the 1960s some pioneering scientists began to focus on these discrepancies where matter or numbers departed from the expected norms, erupting off into what they named "discontinuities," or "bursts of noise."

These did not follow the sequence of mathematics or the rules of the geometries of the past two thousand years; they did not arrange themselves in the classical patterns of lines and planes, circles and spheres. The idealized order of classical science turned out to be the wrong kind of abstraction for understanding complexity, Gleick explained.

The next paragraph was riveting for me. I was immensely excited by the way it described just what I had experienced in my life. I read the next sentences out loud to myself three times: "Clouds are not spheres, Mandlebrot [one of the early chaos scientists] is fond of saying. Mountains are not cones. Lightning does not travel in a straight line. The new geometry mirrors a universe that is rough, not rounded, scabrous, not smooth. It is a geometry of the pitted, pocked, and broken up, the twisted, tangled, and intertwined. . . ."

"Exactly!" I shouted. "That is the texture of the life I know: twisted, tangled, intertwined."

Sitting back down I read on as Gleick described mathematicians and physicists coming upon the reality of chaos. They did not know how to explain it, but there it was. It was so unsettling to the scientific world that attempts to get papers published in professional journals were met with refusal and even contempt. Those who had uncovered chaos were stranded in their discovery, unsure in what direction to proceed.

This disturbed state paralleled a stage I was in for a long time. It was not that I experienced everything as disorder, but it loomed very large for me that disorder was an indisputable fact of life. Life was definitely mixed. Disorder could be counted on to appear on an irregular basis. And often in groups or bunches or crowds.

I noticed, for example, a phenomenon I call the conspiracy of the appliances. I became aware over the years that one appliance never seemed to break down alone. If the refrigerator died just before a slumber party for fifteen sixth-graders, the washing machine could be counted on to whirr ominously, thump, and go still when I was trying to wash the sheets that half of them were sick on in the middle of the night. "Brace for it," I would warn myself, "tomorrow the car won't start when it's time to take them home."

Over the years I developed a kind of wariness. Not a cynicism exactly, just a guardedness. I could no longer be caught unaware. Chaos breaks in.

Jobs can be terminated with little notice. Wonderful people we campaign for may lose political races to creeps. Some Little Leaguer we love very much strikes out with bases loaded.

As I came to know chaos better, I learned it often surfaced at the worst times. After a while I almost expected at least some family members to be sick at Christmas. I identified with a column in our paper in which the columnist, Steve Otto, described his family's holiday illness. He asked: "Have you ever tried Robitussin mixed with eggnog?" I laughed, understanding just what he meant. Even at celebrations, chaos shows up.

Chaos is something that interrupts the flow of life, that breaks into the expected rhythm, that forces us to stop and deal with its difficulty. The seriousness of the chaos depends on the gravity of the threat to what we value in our life.

Some events are inconvenient and annoying, like locking keys in the car, losing material on our computer, or waking up with a cold. Other things are much more serious. Their first signals set off alarms in us that something we cherish deeply may be taken from us. Symptoms of cancer, for example, or an arrest by police, or someone we care about being in a terrible accident—these things can totally change the balance of our world as we know it.

One of the worst features of hard times is that it seems *wrong*, as if these difficulties should not happen. We can feel there must be something the matter with us when bad things happen.

This is a central theme in the Book of Job, a book of the Bible considered to be one of the greatest pieces of ancient literature. It is a reflection on the meaning of suffering.

Job, a very upright and successful man, loses all his possessions, his children, his servants, his health. Friends, family, even Job's wife insist that for this to have happened to Job, he must have done something wrong. He protests that he has been faithful to God. He questions God, arguing that there must be some mistake. These terrible things should not happen to him.

I think it is a natural response in all of us to think that painful events are a mistake. We recoil from the happenings, big and small, that seem unjust or out of the flow of expected sequences of loss. I am reminded of a sad experience recently in the life of my son Boo.

Boo raised a new puppy, a truly wonderful black Labrador retriever. He was all huge feet and ears when Boo first got him, a tumble of black with great dark eyes that would disarm you completely.

Boo, in law school at the time, was studying a famous judge whose decisions and rulings all law students are required to learn. Almost anyone who went to law school would remember this judge because he has a very unusual name; his name is Judge Learned Hand. Boo named his puppy Judge Learned Paw, and called him Judge.

Judge grew bigger than any dog I have ever seen, almost as big as a small pony. Both because Boo is an unusually fine teacher and Judge was exceptionally sweet natured, he was the best behaved dog in my experience. He was patient and obedient, grateful for any attention, insistently, affectionately playful. His eyes were what always got me, eyes that looked right into your soul and let you know—no doubt about it—you were special and he was happy to be sitting by your feet.

Well, in the spring, without any warning, Judge died. A heart attack, it turned out to be. Apparently very big dogs often overstrain their hearts, dying with no preparatory symptoms. He was only five years old.

Boo's wife, Caroline, was home alone with him. She had gone out to get the mail, and came in to find him struggling desperately, then going still. Caroline is tiny. It is hard to imagine how she was able to get that huge dog into their car and to the vet, but she did. The vet examined him immediately, but there was nothing he could do. "He's gone," he said to her. Caroline couldn't believe it.

"It couldn't be true. It's not true," she said, her beautiful green eyes searching his face with the kind of open, disarming goodness she has that makes everyone who meets her love her.

"I'm sure you'll find you've made a mistake. Just look again. You remember, Doctor, this is Judge. Judge couldn't be dead. Look again, I'm sure you'll find he's still breathing. It is just a mistake."

I wept as I heard that story. I understood her response in the deepest part of me. I think we all have that response initially to chaos breaking into our lives: it must be a mistake.

That was the response of the scientific world to the theories of the first chaos scientists.

3

Chaos Has Its Own Time

If you have tohu wa bohu *you know you've got trouble!*

—Carroll Stuhlmueller, C.P.

For a long time I struggled on the outskirts of my own traditional world-view of life, feeling unmoored and isolated. Like editors of scientific journals who refused to publish chaos articles, I thought my difficulties were a mistake and should be fixed or made to go away.

Then one day a great breakthrough happened for me. It was during the time I was associate director of a sabbatical program for people in full-time ministry at the University of Notre Dame.

Sitting in the back of our classroom, I was listening to a deeply respected scripture scholar, Carroll Stuhlmueller, C.P., who was teaching a course for us on the Psalms. I was having a hard time concentrating because major crises were going on in every generation of my family. Various kinds of mental illness were causing cyclones of disturbance on several fronts.

Stuhlmueller was saying that the praise psalms were praising God for creation, and often for creation in the sense of deliverance from some kind of turmoil. My focus sharpened when I heard the word turmoil.

He said that the concept of creation for the biblical people was never creation out of nothing (as we commonly think of it), but always *creation out of chaos.*

He told us that the Hebrew word for chaos was *tohu wa bohu.* "Doesn't it really sound like what it is?" he asked. "If you have something called *tohu wa bohu,* you know you've got trouble!"

He explained that those ancient people considered chaos always to be lurking on the edge of creation, ready to take it over at any moment.

Stuhlmueller's class had a profound effect on me. Perhaps due to the power of timing, I was comforted at a very fundamental level. I felt deeply reassured that there was not necessarily something wrong with me if life seemed on the edge of chaos. That is just the way things are and *always* have been. Hearing that this was the experience of the biblical peoples, that it is the pattern of the scriptures, really consoled me. It helped me to know that my story was their story. I was freed to see the chaos, the *tohu wa bohu,* as an objective reality, as a normal part of life.

Chaos scientists gradually brought the scholarly world to accept the same conclusion. In laboratory experiments and measurements of real life phenomena like weather turbulence, epidemics, or population growth, suddenly there may be discontinuities. What had seemed predictable based on the classic view of laws of nature will not always happen. Something else may. Chaos erupts. That is just the way things are.

Accepting that chaos was just a part of life brought me to a radically revised comprehension of the rhythm of things. I heard with new resonance the ancient poetry of Ecclesiastes 3:

There is a season for everything, a time for every
occupation under heaven:
A time for giving birth,
a time for dying. . . .
a time for mourning,
a time for dancing.

In the midst of all the different rhythms and seasons, contrasts and turnings of human life for thousands of years, I understood that chaos also has a time.

I thought of a phrase from an exchange I had with Catherine Mason, my closest neighbor when I lived in South Bend. She was 91, a marvelous woman. She walked a mile each way to Mass every morning on the Notre Dame campus, she played bridge every week, she wrote to her children and grandchildren and great-grandchildren. She cleaned out her garage. For all I know she turned her mattress once a month.

On this particular day, I was washing my nine-year-old car, getting ready to sell it. I was crying as I washed it because it was the last car that had belonged to Dad and Mom, the last one they both drove before they got too sick to drive. As I emptied the glove compartment I found things I had forgotten were in there, like the bill of sale with Dad's signature and a notebook with records of gas mileage and oil changes in Mom's writing.

Catherine came by and stopped to talk, and I told her it was hard for me to say good-bye to the old Volkswagen, and she said slowly, "There comes a time."

I was very moved by that. She said it with the seasoned poignancy of someone who has said good-bye to many things—to her husband, to the big, old house where they had raised their eight children, to many of her friends. "There comes a time." Planting and uprooting the plant. Building and tearing down. Keeping and casting away. Embracing and being far from embraces.

There are seasons, I said to myself, and there's not something wrong with us that some of those seasons are for difficult, chaotic events. Chaos has a time of its own.

Not long ago we had an extended season in our family of progressing illnesses and increasing helplessness of all the older generation. Our parents and some beloved aunts, uncles, and cousins who had never had children of their own looked to my sisters and me for many levels of support. One by one, over several years, they died. The last and dearest of those we accompanied on this part of their journey were Mom and Dad. They died just five months apart.

The final year was hard for both of them, the simplest things becoming a challenge: breathing, turning over, swallowing. I don't know which was worse, Dad, with Alzheimer's disease, being so confused, so unable to bring his own great mind to bear on his suffering; or Mom, still perfectly alert, knowing everything, her understanding exposing her to the terror of the collapse of her own body within her.

Mom died in the summer, and then, after a long and painful autumn, Dad died too. In his last weeks he was very confused and agitated, and what I remember the most are his hands. He had beautiful hands, strong and well shaped, with long, expressive fingers.

Mom, whose hands were small and square with short, unpoetic fingers, used to point out Dad's hands to the three of us when we were growing up. "Look at your father's hands, girls," she would say, "doesn't he have beautiful hands?" In the end those hands were very restless, the fingers endlessly plucking at his blankets.

It was December 21 that his hands came to rest at last. A few days later we gathered in the rain at the military cemetery by the Tennessee River, watching his casket being lowered into the ground next to the stone with Mom's name on it. A soldier with a trumpet played "Taps" with slow, aching gentleness, its notes the sound of the ending of the day, of a life, of a generation, of a long family sequence of deaths.

A few days later marked the new year. I returned to the University of Notre Dame where I was working, feeling bewildered and disconnected. Orphaned, even at fifty.

In May I drove back home to Florida where I spent the summers in the house where I had raised my children. The trip was painful for me, filled with a stark awareness that I would not be stopping to see Mom and Dad as I drove back. What had been the pattern for a long time, breaking the trip for a good visit with them, would not be the pattern from now on.

In the sense that they had symbolized "home" all my life long, I could never go home again.

When I arrived at my house late the next day I discovered that my daughter Kadee was pregnant. She had waited for me to return to tell me the news in person. She and John had been married seven years. That very day of my return she had been to the doctor and had a sonogram which she showed to me.

I was absolutely awestruck. Looking at a picture of your first grandchild within the womb of your own first-born is an extraordinary experience. I felt a huge shift inside me. A new pattern was forming. The sonogram revealed that the baby was a boy. He was due in the fall, nine months after my father's death.

When the baby was born, I flew down from Notre Dame to see him and pulled up in their yard just as they drove in from the hospital. Kadee was holding him in her arms in a soft white blanket, and the first thing I saw were his hands. Long hands for a baby. Beautifully shaped. Fine, long fingers that were plucking at his blanket. . . . Tears streamed down my face. Life and death and now—here—life again. For everything there is a season. Chaos and then . . . creation.

4

Creation Out of Chaos

In profound appreciation of the boll weevil. . . .

—Roy Shoffner

The realization that chaos is part of life, like a season that comes and goes, I think of as stage three of my attempt to understand the dynamic of struggle.

Stage one was the foundational period of stability and order that seemed to define how life should be. Stage two was the frightening discovery of chaos. Life was not orderly (mine at least) and something was very wrong with that. Stage three began with the realization that chaos is part of life with recurring seasons. In this stage I was able to rethink in a new light some things that had happened.

An example of this rethinking was the new perspective from which I began to see a bizarre occurrence that impacted me deeply even though I did not hear the story for years after it occurred.

When the children were small we owned a piece of land out in the country that included pasture for cows and a couple of horses. There were a few old grapefruit trees where the animals would gather in the shade. (The trees were so well fertilized by the livestock that they bore the sweetest fruit in the county!)

Next to this pasture, way down a rutted drive, was the homestead of an old farmer. It had a frame house with a tin roof and a big porch. A few hundred yards from the house was the original old barn, weathered for decades, leaning perilously to one side, its grayed wood gnarled and gapped.

My son Randy was out early on a Saturday morning with his BB gun looking for adventures. (I was adamantly opposed to BB guns, but in his father's view, they were a totally non-negotiable feature of boyhood in the rural central Florida culture.) That morning Randy had been shooting at fence posts and grapefruit, but since there wasn't much challenge in shooting things that did not move, he was looking for better prey.

Suddenly he spotted a dragonfly going over the neighbor's fence. What a target! He squeezed through the fence and stalked the dragonfly as it made its way toward the barn and settled on the horseshoe over the barn door. He sighted the gun and shot, missing the dragonfly, but hitting the horseshoe with a satisfying ping. "Cool," he said to himself, beginning to grin.

Then he heard a terrible creaking sound. The leaning barn began to lurch before his eyes, monstrously stirring, shifting, losing its hold on the edge of balance, on the brim of gravity. With a noise of great straining and cracking the barn fell into a huge heap of splintered wood, dust dimming the bright morning air. In total terror Randy took off, through the fence, across the pasture, up the road, never looking back.

It was ten years before he even told me the story.

The falling barn is a very vivid image for me. When I first heard it, the meaning it had for me was one of fragility. How perilous life is. How we weather and lean in the storms and misuses and hard, long years of our hearts and beings. And then one day, one hostile hit, one unkindness, one act mostly unintended, can cause our collapse. The good luck horseshoe over the doorway becomes a target even though the aim was at something else.

Seen in that light, the collapse of the barn seemed almost unbearably sad, and something in me wanted to run up the road and not look back.

It was after my neighbor, Catherine Mason, at 91, commented on my painful selling of my parent's VW with her wonderful line, "There comes a time . . ." that I thought of the barn story again. Without trying to (who knows how these things happen?) I played it again in my mind. My imagination went back to the moment of the falling barn and painted a different ending.

This time I pictured Randy not running. I pictured him telling himself he had to face the music. I saw him in my mind's eye squaring his shoulders and walking through the dust cloud to the road up to the farmer's house. In my picture the farmer was on his front porch drinking water from a Mason jar in the hot morning, wiping his face with an old white handkerchief.

I saw Randy scuffing the toe of his sneaker in the dust, taking a big breath, and confessing what had happened—pointing with his BB gun at the barn collapsed in the distance.

I saw the man's intense blue eyes in his lined brown face take the measure of Randy. He looked at him hard and long, saying nothing. Finally he spit some water off the side of the porch into the dust and said: "Good shot, son. You put that old barn out of its misery."

I was amazed at the new version. It really had a profound effect on me, one I needed badly in a year of deaths and other painful endings. There comes a time. Endings are not all bad. There is not something wrong with us, not something wrong with life. Things sometimes need to end. "You put it out of its misery," I said to myself in the voice of the old farmer, and I began to laugh.

This was the beginning of my really planting myself in stage three of my understanding. Life is not predictable and orderly, it is laced with unexpected difficulties. This is not a mistake. Discontinuity is a characteristic of reality.

In fact, the humorous image of the fallen barn and the insight that sometimes it is *good* for things to end, helped me move farther in a direction that had been already slowly opening in my mind. I was entering the fourth and current stage of my understanding.

I began to have a conviction that chaos and creation did not just co-exist in reality, but that sometimes chaos is the *raw material* of creation. The *tohu wa bohu* is not necessarily evil. Perhaps creation is not the product of combat between good and evil, as many primitive myths portray, resulting in a very closely contested victory for the forces of Good.

Chaos is energy and power, untamed and unformed, but not bad. It can be shaped and channeled, tamed and reinterpreted in ways that bring new creation to life.

Something may need to die before something else can be born. Something new may come into being, something better, fresher than we had ever hoped for or imagined.

A fascinating example of this dynamic was pointed out to me when I was visiting my son Boo. He was stationed at Ft. Rucker, Alabama, and he and Caroline lived in the nearby town of Enterprise. They were giving me the grand tour of the post and the town, and stopped in the middle of the little downtown to show me a famous landmark statue. "It is the only monument in the world to an insect," Boo said, dryly, waiting for me to comment.

"An insect?"

"Take a look." He drove close to the white statue on a tall pedestal in the middle of a fountain. The statue was of a woman draped in Grecian style holding over her head . . . a *bug*!!

"What in the world is it?"

"A boll weevil, Mom. Here's the story. This area was a one crop farm area, like most of the South. The crop was cotton. When the boll weevils came up from Mexico in 1915, almost the whole crop was destroyed.

"This all but paralyzed the economy of the county and the surrounding areas. The farmers were unable to pay their bills, merchants were caught in the squeeze and couldn't meet their obligations, bankers were caught with loans that could not be called in.

"H. M. Sessions, a banker who had advanced money on the crop to many farmers, began to preach diversification of crops. This was a pitch for the wisdom of having more than one potential source of income. In addition or instead of cotton, he suggested raising corn, or livestock, or maybe peanuts, a crop that was beginning to be grown and sold for many different purposes.

"Farmers were reluctant to give up farming cotton, because it was all they knew. Generations before them had grown it on this same land. Only a few tried diversifying the first year, but with the continued disaster the weevil brought the second year, most began to change to different crops, particularly peanuts.

"The farmers of Enterprise not only regained their losses, but they prospered as never before. As it turns out, cotton is a very labor intensive crop. The money and effort it takes to produce a living in cotton is far greater than for a crop like peanuts.

"And so it was decided," Boo concluded in his tour guide voice, "to dedicate a monument on this spot where we are today."

Getting out of the car, I walked over and read the inscription on the base: "In profound appreciation of the boll weevil and what it has done as the herald of prosperity, this monument was erected by the citizens of Enterprise, Coffee County, Alabama, in the year of Our Lord 1919."

Clearly, I said to myself, creation out of chaos. I stood there for a long time looking at the monument, thinking about life.

Over and over, now that my ear is tuned to the music of this dance, I hear these stories. I heard a man say: "When I went bankrupt, I discovered that life was about love, not money."

My friend Lona said, "When I got hit by a truck while riding my bicycle my back was broken. As strange as it sounds, in my terrible recovery I learned to savor joy."

"When my son got in trouble with drugs," one woman told me, "I thought it was the end of the world. But in his recovery process, he discovered God and himself."

There seems to be a pattern here if we look hard enough, if we listen carefully enough.

This is what the chaos scientists discovered as well. If they ran the chaotic numbers long enough through the computers, if they observed the experiments long enough in the laboratories, they found a pattern in the results.

There was a consistent configuration in the plotting of the results they called "a strange attractor." There was a pattern in the distribution of the numbers that was a constant. This was true no matter what the content of the chaos observed was: population growths, turbulence in weather, dripping faucets, or epidemics. A perplexing pattern emerged deep in the chaos.

There is a pattern like this at the heart of the Judeo-Christian revelation. Like the inexplicable strange attractor or mathematical constant, it is the ever recurring mystery that is the theme of scripture and the theme of each human life. It is the pattern of life from death. Liberation from bondage. Resurrection after crucifixion.

Year after year, spring follows winter. A baby is born with the hands of the grandfather. There is at the heart of being a constant force for life, a force that brings creation out of chaos.

This seems to me to be the answer to my long ago cry: "Where is God in all of this?" The force for life is at the heart of the mystery of God. There is blessing in the mess.

5

Grappling With Mystery

For remember, the one undeniably true statement
that we can make about God is that God is mystery.
So we are people engaged in grappling with mystery,
or perhaps better, people with whom mystery is
grappling.

—Michael Himes

The birth of my first grandchild nine months after the funeral
of my father was one of a series of significant events that dra-
matically shifted the family focus from death to new life. In less
than three years there were three weddings and five births.

My son Randy married after outlasting all his backwoods,
central Florida boyhood friends in bachelorhood. He chose a
perfectly wonderful young woman named Silvia whose mother is from Panama and father from Argentina, a woman of both
innocence and great strength, both prayerful and playful. He
was 28 and she was 19. The first time I met her I said to myself:
"*There* is the smile that will win the heart of the bachelor
prince." And it did.

A year later they were waiting for their baby to be born.
The due date had already passed. Silvia had a doctor's appoint-
ment in the morning, and she got a call from her mother asking
to go with her. Her mother was worried. They were together

in the examining room as the doctor looked at Silvia. "Everything's fine," said the doctor, rising to leave after a cursory check.

"It is not fine," said Silvia's mother. "Something is wrong. Something is very wrong, I know it." The doctor gave her an indignant look as if to say "Who is the doctor here anyway?"

Silvia's mother looked straight back at him. "I have had six babies," she said, "and been involved with the birth of many more. Something is not right. I think you should induce the baby."

The doctor was incensed. "There are no signs of anything wrong. She is only a few days overdue. I have no intention of inducing this baby."

"Then there must at least be a sonogram to check things out," she countered, not giving an inch. He made an impatient noise, and condescendingly agreed that one be scheduled for the next morning.

The nurse doing the sonogram turned pale when she looked at the picture, left the room and ran to call the doctor. There was no amniotic fluid left at all. The baby was in great distress, moments from death.

They rushed Silvia to delivery for an emergency C-section, calling Randy to come right away. Randy is a registered nurse (an amazing story in itself), so he could scrub up and be there.

For cesarean section deliveries, they put a partition or curtain between the mother's head and her abdomen so she doesn't see herself being cut open. Randy was on Silvia's side of the curtain, holding her hands. The doctor pulled out the baby, and there was just silence. Randy ducked around the curtain to see. The baby was a beautiful boy. But he was blue, not breathing at all.

Silvia called out: "What is it? Is the baby OK? What's happening?" Randy came back around the curtain and took her in his arms and they began to pray. Moments stretched. They heard a little cough. And then a whimper. Then slowly, gaining in strength, a long, loud wail.

Randy ran back around the curtain and they handed him the baby.

"Looks like a Jacob to me," he said, "Wrestled with God's angel and lived." He brought the baby to Silvia.

Jacob is now three years old. I just got back from spending the night with that little family where they live 100 miles from me. Jacob, perfectly healthy, was dancing the Macarena in his red pajamas in the middle of the living room.

There is a very deep truth that we learn in life contained in the story of Jacob struggling all night with the angel, found in the Book of Genesis (32:26-32). We have moments of wrestling with God. "Grappling with mystery," theologian Michael Himes says, or, more accurately, "moments when mystery grapples with us."

This Old Testament image is very helpful to me in my attempt to understand God and chaos.

Things happen, as I have said, that we do not understand—unwelcome events like illnesses and accidents, injustices and disappointments, the loss of jobs, the death of dreams. Rejections that send us sprawling on the pavement of our world. We lose people we love and we can't seem to get rid of people who drive us crazy.

Life gets hold of us in the guise of difficult people we must strain against and circumstances that disrupt our peace. It helps me to think of these people and these events as mystery grappling with me. In the Judeo-Christian tradition we name the mystery "God."

I mentioned earlier the archetypal biblical story of Job as the tale of someone trying to understand suffering. After years of spectacular blessing, he has lost everything.

The news of his losses one after another—of his cattle, his sheep and shepherds, his camels, his servants, his children—comes to him with a terrible refrain. Each time a messenger announces the disaster with the words: "They are all dead, I alone escaped to tell you."

After the losses, Job has continuing torments: Satan afflicting him with horrible sores, until he is sitting on a dung heap being licked by dogs. His wife and his friends taunt him that it must be his own fault, that he must have sinned. Job curses the day he was born in wrenching lament. Then passage follows passage devoted to the exploration of the problem of suffering.

The only answer given is that it is mystery. God responds to Job's questions with questions. In the magnificent poetry of chapters 38 and 39, God shows how far beyond Job's comprehension is the scope of the work of the Creator:

Were you there when I laid the earth's foundations . . .
when all the stars of morning were singing with joy? (38:4, 6)

Have you ever in your life given orders to the morning
or sent the dawn to its post? (38:12)

Have you ever visited the place where the snow is
kept or seen where the hail is stored up? (38:22)

Does the hawk take flight on your advice
when he spreads his wings to travel south?
Does the eagle soar at your command
to make her eyrie in the heights? (39:26-27)

The message is clear: God's ways are not ours, God's wisdom is mysterious, manifest in divine works. Job at last accepts this truth and stops struggling:

"My words have been frivolous . . .
I will not speak again. (40:4, 5)

I have been holding forth on matters I cannot understand,
on marvels beyond me and my knowledge." (42:3)

He drops his angry protestations, acknowledging that "the one who made the morning" has ways he cannot understand. He comes to a new place within himself that is more than resignation. It is an enlarged sense of the dimension of life with God. It is an elemental trust.

I believe this is a place to which we are all called. But I am also convinced that no one arrives there easily. Significant wrestling in the dark with God like Jacob, or shouting from the dung heap like Job, are required for that enlargement. In our anguish we throw the force of our passion back against God, objecting, lamenting.

A young couple I know have a baby boy who was born without most of his intestines. After two years he is still in the hospital, the chances of his ever having a normal life very much in question. They are with him every day, their hearts wrung by his beautiful little self, walking and talking, hugging and charming, but totally dependent on tubes to live.

The father, a hard-working young attorney, is a physical giant. He has charisma that fills the room when he walks in. I was not surprised to learn that he was once the U.S. amateur champion heavyweight boxer of the U.S. At a recent brunch gathering, in the midst of talking about his son, he put down his fork and looked at each of us, demanding in a voice taut with pain: "Is life just a cruel joke? *Is it*!?! I need to know!"

This time he is in the ring with mystery.

When Jacob wrestled with the angel, the struggle went on all through the night. At daybreak, when the angel tried to disengage by dislocating Jacob's hip, Jacob refused to give up, insisting: "I will not let go unless you bless me."

The angel (representing God) blesses him and gives him a new name. He will be called Israel, one who is strong with God. Jacob leaves the encounter limping, but knowing he will have the blessing forever.

This can be a turning point in the lives of all of us. In one way or another, early in life or late, with forces inside of us or outside of us, we are flung to the ground in the grip of mystery.

We struggle with all our might, and in the midst of our passion-
ate defense, we may discover not a cruel joke, but a blessing.
We may learn that the grappling can end in grace.

6

The Blessing in the Struggle

On those who dwelt in the land of deep shadow,
a light has shone.

—Isaiah 9:1

I have come to believe that the most important creation out of chaos may be precisely the blessing that comes out of the long night of struggling with mystery.

Only after many rounds in the ring have I finally been able to let go of the kind of primitive assumption that if God is with me I will be spared from trouble.

It has become clearer to me how skewed (though thoroughly and touchingly understandable) is our typical response when we survive disaster. Many people who escaped uninjured in recent tornadoes in Florida, for example, said: "God really had a hand on us."

This seems to imply that if there had been injury or death, it would mean that God had let go, that God was somehow indifferent. Or, worse, had directly intended the harming.

I feel certain that God does not *cause* bad things to happen to us. God is not tormenting us, or capriciously subjecting us to demonstrations of power, or testing us from some perch high above us to see how much we can stand. How could this be a loving God?

We are faced with the fact, however, that God plainly created a universe in which struggle would be inevitable. It is a universe where the dynamics of physics will sometimes lead to catastrophe in nature (such as tornadoes), and the dynamic of free will sometimes leads to catastrophe within and between people (such as sin, crime, and war).

I once thought these were just sort of unfortunate side effects of the law of cause and effect, just the price we must pay for the gift of human freedom.

Now I see also that struggle can be the milieu in which further creation occurs. Without some experience of significant challenge we might never discover what really matters in life. "Without a hurt the heart is hollow," the musical *The Fantastics* proclaims in its song "Try to Remember."

Like the Native American custom of the vision quest, life happenings of great magnitude drive us into the wilderness of our own inner being, cut us off from the familiar world we take for granted, and force us to explore our own souls. Who are we really? What is it all about?

In a workshop I attended recently, psychologist Martin Helldorfer offered a session on betrayal. He described the dynamic of betrayal, and underscored the fact that it is normal in human life to be betrayed at some time by another person (parent, spouse, friend, child, colleague), by an institution (church, company, country), or by a cause.

Then he said something I had not been expecting. He said that betrayal is crucial if we are ever to grow up. We must lose our primitive, archaic, childlike trust that nothing bad will ever happen to us. We remain unformed if we are never forced to enter the reality of imperfection, thrown back deep into ourselves on resources of which we are only dimly aware. Carl Jung calls this painful process "individuation." It is suggested in Jesus' saying that we must lose our lives to gain them. Helldorfer asserted that "Betrayal is an invitation to growth, depth, awareness, a living spirituality." There is no new life without some form of death. Betrayal can, in the end, be blessing.

There is a powerful line at the end of Peter Beagle's lovely book, *The Last Unicorn*: "Great heroes need great sorrows and burdens, or half their greatness goes unnoticed."

"So who wants to be great, anyway?" we grumble. "Greatness is overvalued!" The One who loves us in freedom and mystery calls us to greatness, knowing that if we knew the price we would hardly choose it on our own.

For me, greatness begins to be created in the discovery in the wilderness, at the edge of my limits, that I am not alone. The One who is with me is Love.

Love-with-me does not mean that I have some magic charm that will make my wishes come true, that will shield me from ever being injured. It means I have infinite value, that my life is an invitation to share in creative love, and that this deeply mysterious Other who is the source of all being, the beginning and end of all life, is closer than my own heart.

After Jacob's night of wrestling with the angel he named the place Peniel which means "the face of God," "because I have seen God face to face and I have survived." My experience of these times of trial is that if transformation takes place in me it is precisely because in some way it has been an experience of seeing God face to face. I don't mean this in any sense of a physical apparition, but of a *knowing* and *being known*.

This was the "pearl of great price," as the gospel of Mathew calls it, the gift I was given no matter what happened in the particular crisis that threw me into the ring. It was as if the most important thing were not the outcome, but the fact that in the struggle I received the blessing.

During a recent workshop someone told me this story:

*There was a terrible storm one night with very loud
thunder, huge bolts of lightning, wind howling and toppling
things over. The next morning dawned bright and clear. A
little girl in town told her mom how terrified she had been.
She asked her mother: "What was God doing during the
storm?" While the mother was groping around for an*

43

answer, the little girl said, "I know! God was making the morning!"

Slowly over time I have gotten better at trusting that in storm-wracked times God is making a morning. The morning is not necessarily the answer I was hoping for, or any answer or resolution; but the morning is a new ability to trust even though I do not understand. That very trust is like the dawning of a light in what had been impenetrable night.

I am always moved at Christmas by the scriptural images of light and darkness from the readings of the prophet Isaiah and the gospel of John: From Isaiah 9 we read: "The people who walked in darkness have seen a great light; upon those who dwelt in the land of deep shadow, a light has shone." In the first chapter of John we hear: "The light shone in the darkness and the darkness did not overcome it."

Four Decembers ago was a frightening time in my family. My first grandchild was two months old, and the pediatrician was concerned that there was something seriously wrong with his skull. She feared that the openings in the bone plates, the spaces we call the soft spots, were not formed right, and that his head would not grow and his brain would be damaged. His mother, my daughter Kadee, had terrible post-partum depression and was valiantly struggling for the courage to deal with this awful threat.

I was with her and the baby at Walker Memorial, a Seventh Day Adventist hospital in their town, waiting to get X-rays in time to be mailed overnight to a specialist before all medical offices shut down for the holidays. There was real time pressure because if this condition were not treated before he was three months old, the damage would be irreversible.

The X-ray department was overcrowded and understaffed and the waiting room was filled with people trying to get X-rays before the holiday closings. Most of the people were over seventy, many in considerable pain. We had been there nearly an hour, and the baby cried and cried no matter what we did.

The people in the waiting room kept saying things like: "What is wrong with him?" "Why don't you feed him?" "Why don't you change him?" "What are you doing to him?" "Is there a diaper pin stuck in him?" My attempt to say clearly, "Babies just cry sometimes, it's part of every day!" was met with disbelieving stares.

Finally my daughter was too agitated to sit there any longer, and she went outside the hospital to get some air. I took the baby to walk up and down the corridor, close to tears with helplessness and frustration and terror at what the X-rays might reveal. The spectre of surgery on the tiny head of this precious child or his being brain damaged forever plunged me into the dark.

I don't know what made me look up as I paced the corridor with him, his cries echoing to every corner of the floor. Framed on the wall were pictures of the days of creation, the seven days the Adventists reverence deeply. I was by Day One. I saw a great sunburst in primal colors and the words printed so clearly it was as if I heard them spoken: "Let there be light."

"'The light shone in the darkness,'" I said to myself, "'and the darkness did not overcome it.' Christmas Eve is tomorrow. God is with us." I looked down and saw that the baby, little Forrest Lee, had fallen asleep. "Upon those who dwelt in the land of deep shadow, a light has shone."

We did not find out for several weeks that the X-rays showed his head, though somewhat crookedly shaped, was normal. His brain has been growing ever since, outwitting us at many a turn.

I was more grateful than I can possibly say for this outcome. But my gratitude was for even more than the huge relief that little Forrest's head did not have to be cut open. The even greater blessing was that, in the midst of not knowing whether there would have to be surgery or not, there was a light that the darkness would not be able to put out. The light was an illuminated reassurance deep inside me that, *no matter what*, we were in the arms of Love.

Only in the chaos of darkness can the real power of that light shine. The blessing is the ultimate revelation that—now and always—God is with us.

I will always remember how the blessing came to me in that hospital corridor. I return to the moment in my mind as a great treasure each time chaos blows through my front door and I am afraid once more.

7

The Grip of Fear

Fear is the razor edge of chaos.

—Martha Lakis

The long nights of grappling with mystery leave us wounded, yet, like Jacob, strangely blessed. I believe this with my whole heart, and yet I also need to say quickly that the next time chaos comes I am afraid all over again.

I am reminded of an afternoon when I was outside watching my grandson and suddenly saw a snake. My whole body froze in the laser focus of acute danger. I desperately tried to recall the rhyme all country Florida children learn to remember the difference between the harmless king snake and the deadly coral snake. Both have bands of red, yellow, and black, but the colors alternate in a different order.

"Red-on-yellow, kill a fellow; red-on-black, your friend, Jack," I repeated soundlessly to myself. This snake, five feet away from where my little grandson was playing with his toy cars on the front step, was definitely red-on-yellow. I have been told that a toddler would have little chance of surviving the bite of a coral snake.

A shovel was leaning against the side of the house where I could stretch to reach it, moving more quietly than ever in my whole life, trying not to warn the snake. I closed my fingers around the shovel handle. Worse than having this snake where

I knew where it was would be having it dart under the house where I didn't know where it was.

I raised the shovel slowly in the air and brought it down on the snake in one breath, chopping it in half. The baby kept playing, making his little car sounds, paying no attention. The contrast of his trusting movements and the halves of the deadly snake still coiling under the shovel made me so weak I had to sit on the ground.

Poisonous snakes are a metaphor for all that I fear. Fear is a huge counterforce in the ongoing attempt to learn to trust God. It is, for me, one of the worst currents of chaos.

Fear can be deadly. When very anxious about something in my own life, or something in the life of someone I love, I can allow it to control my whole world. The dread spreads cold and heavy through the center of me, brutally blocking all lightheartedness. It erodes my ability to enjoy the simplest things, shuts down laughter, and robs me of peace. It stalks me in the middle of the night.

The summer of helping my mother die was unforgettable. Being with her in the messiness, the pain, the fury, the loss of dignity, the misery, the utter powerlessness that dying can be, the worst of it all was her fear. And our fear for her. She really wanted to die, but she still could not escape the fear. It came for her like a demon.

When she could not get her breath from the emphysema, she appeared to be taken over by a primitive panic so strong that it overwhelmed any desire she had to let go.

The area of the brain that has developed systems over countless millennia to keep the body alive seemed to send out signals of terrible alarm when she was threatened with extinction. She could not control the part of her that was built to fight for life; her fear was like a smoke alarm that goes off in a church because it can't distinguish incense from arson.

When we are threatened in some significant way, we cannot avoid being frightened. For some time now I have been struggling with how to deal with fear in my life. It has been life-giving to grasp from the scripture that the Spirit of God not only does not cause fear, but longs to relieve our fear (Romans 8:14-15).

"Do not be afraid," I heard a scripture scholar say, is perhaps the most characteristic salutation, greeting or response of God or messengers of God in the Bible, Old Testament and New. Over and over again in situations that are difficult, bleak, or overwhelming, scripture reveals God as saying, as is written in Isaiah 43, "Do not be afraid for I am with you. Do not be afraid, for I have redeemed you; I have called you by your name, you are mine."

No matter how trying or terrifying the situation in which we find ourselves, we are assured that God is with us, saving us, cherishing us, wanting to break fear's hold on us. Yet fear's hold can be fierce.

I have made some progress at reaching for trust when I am terribly afraid. I think this is because I have had many frightening times in which I found God trustworthy. Not that bad things did not happen, not that some magical solution occurred, but that there was a sense, somehow, sometime in the struggle, that God did not abandon me. As in the hospital corridor with my tiny grandson, in the midst of the threat came a blessing.

There was a particularly helpful passage in a book. For some weeks a couple of years ago I began my day by reading a few pages of Anthony DeMello's *One Minute Wisdom*. The chapters are dialogues between a spiritual master and his disciple. One page that resonated with me very deeply began with the disciple asking the master:

> *"What is the greatest enemy of enlightenment?"*
> *"Fear."*
> *"And where does fear come from?"*
> *"Delusion."*
> *"And what is delusion?"*

> *nat the flowers around you are*
> *nus snakes."*
> *......ni I attain Enlightenment?"*
> *"Open your eyes and see."*
> *"What?"*
> *"That there isn't a single snake around."*

I talked to my great friend Mary about this passage in the days that followed. We changed the ending a little, because at that time in our lives we felt there were definitely snakes around coiling to strike. Our paraphrase of how we might somehow attain enlightenment was this:

> *"Open your eyes and see."*
> *"What?"*
> *"That because God is with us, no matter what*
> *happens, somehow the snakes become flowers."*

Snakes becoming flowers, poison transformed into beauty, is an accurate image for me of the dynamic described in Chapter Four, of creation coming out of chaos. What we fear turns out to bring a gift. What seems deadly, flowers with new life. The boll weevil was the herald of prosperity in Alabama.

A snakes-becoming-flowers example unfolds in the story in Genesis of Joseph and the coat of many colors. Sold by his brothers to be taken into slavery in Egypt, he was able to save his whole family from famine years later because in Egypt he had become chief steward to the Pharaoh.

A contemporary example appears in the book of Joseph Cardinal Bernadin of Chicago, *The Gift of Peace*, published after his death. In the handwritten introduction, Bernadin asserts that the terrible events of his last years, false accusation of sexual misconduct and terminal cancer, turned out to be gifts. In spite of the humiliation, pain, and fear, "the reconciliation, love, pastoral sensitivity and peace" given him showed how "God can write straight with crooked lines." He wrote: "Though the good and bad are always present in our human condition . . . if we 'let go' in the hands of the Lord, the good will prevail."

Examples from human life of the pattern of goodness coming out of great difficulty are important to me. They reduce the fear inherent in chaos. I am also grateful for examples of the dynamic of forces of destruction leading to new life which can be seen in nature. Fires in the wilderness are often necessary to clear out undergrowth that can choke a healthy forest. Monsoons which cause so much terrible damage in Bangladesh are the crucial source of rain for the crop lands of central India. Severe drought and famine would occur without the monsoons.

There are many manifestations of the dynamic of good coming out of harm, of snakes turning into flowers, of creation out of chaos again and again. Seeing this pattern, trying to trust it, is what helps me the most with the fear that can cripple me in chaos.

However, I can still get very frightened and I have a long way to go to enlightenment! There was a period of fear in our family some time ago, and I tell myself the story whenever I need encouragement. It had to do with head lice.

Head lice definitely qualifies as chaos. An article I read (I researched practically everything written) in the *Boston Globe* by columnist Irene Sege said:

> *In my experience there are three kinds of parents*
> *of young children: those who will never forget*
> *when their children had lice, those whose children*
> *are currently infested, and those who dread*
> *becoming members of either group. There are 12*
> *million cases a year.*

It was the first time I have personally had to deal with head lice. I discovered they have been very bad all over the country these past few years. I have friends in Indiana whose daughter's school began having each student put his or her coat in a plastic bag at the start of the day to protect them from possible infestation from other coats.

Paul, the dad of the little girl, is a musician. He wrote a song about lice and sang it at the school assembly to keep up everyone's spirits. At the end of the year he wrote and taught his daughter's second grade class an opera called *Our Friends, the Lice* in which his daughter had the role of "the head louse." This was his contribution to taming the fear every family had experienced!

The worst part of lice is the shame. As if there is something filthy about you, something degraded, something guilty and horribly culpable about you if you have head lice in your family. So you shrink from asking where the lice shampoos are kept in the drug store, and clandestinely search and re-search every aisle. Looking dignified, putting on a good front, you look the other way, whistling, when you put the products down on the counter, acting casual, like it was Colgate, or Tylenol P.M. When you get home you work around the clock to get rid of them before you will have to tell people.

This is ridiculous. Head lice are no more shameful than chicken pox and far less life threatening. However, they are a crushing amount of work: vacuuming, washing everything that they could have come in contact with in the hottest water, going through the hair strand by strand.

(I need to point out that by now you are probably itching. I can never think about head lice without itching. Just keep in mind: you were not itching before I started on this, you definitely do not have them.)

My daughter Kadee got them from a neighbor family whose kids brought them home from school. Her hair has always been her glory. Ever since she was old enough to decide the issue, she has worn it very long. It is dark and thick with a natural wave that means she never has to do anything but wash it and let it dry. Through all her seasons of wrestling with the heartbreaks and breakdowns of life, at least she had her hair.

What we finally concluded after rounds of battling the problem was that the hair was going to have to get cut. We simply couldn't defeat the lice in that waist length mass. It was terrible for her, really dreadful. Almost like an amputation of a limb. Her physical sense of herself was deeply rooted in her long hair. It was a horrible day.

Something happened so unexpectedly that I still can't think about it without getting a catch in my throat. The afternoon we had to cut her hair, she and I and my dear friend Mary from South Bend were out in the carport. Mary had come to Florida with her girls for a New Year's vacation, and she called me to see if we could get together. When I told her we were struggling with this awful lice thing, she said "I will come help you. My girls have had them. I remember what do to." (Is this not an incredible friend who will give up three days on the beach in January and drive 100 miles to confront the enemy of lice? What a person to have in your corner!)

So on this day we had been facing the inevitability of my daughter's hair having to be cut, and we all felt the dread and the vulnerability. Mary said: "I'll be the one to do it, it is better for you to hate me than your mom. How short can you stand it?" Kadee pulled her hair together in her hand at the back of her neck, saying "Please, no shorter than this."

Mary put her hand over Kate's and began to cut. I held a big plastic bag over the length of it to catch it when it fell. If I live to be a hundred years old I will always be able to hear the sound of those scissors through her hair.

What Mary and I saw when the last of the hair was cut through horrified us. Without realizing it, with her hand over Kadee's, she had been holding the hair on an angle, and the hair on the top had been cut way up, chopped on the angle half way up the back of Kadee's head. Mary's eyes met mine in panic. "We are in for it now! How can we ever fix this?"

And then the hair swung forward. Since it had been pulled straight back from Kadee's face, the hair in the front was much longer than the back and it came forward softly along her jaw framing her face, angled on a slant to the back, cut up in the back in a perfect wedge. It was, in fact, the very hair-do that was so much in style! It looked like a $100 5th Avenue designer cut. Sophisticated and perky, elegant and swinging free, the most becoming haircut of her life!

And as it turned out, the task was almost simple once the hair was short. It was not too hard to go through it all. She was rid of the lice from that afternoon on. Everywhere she went people said: "Kadee, your hair is darling. Stunning. Why haven't you gotten it cut years ago? So who did it for you?" "Oh," she said, "A friend of my mom's. A wonderful friend. A kind of magical person who comes and turns terrible things into something good."

I called Mary to tell her what Kadee said, and she responded "It was one of those times of Mystery, wasn't it?"

"Yes," I replied. "A time of snakes and flowers." She knew what I meant.

8

The Gift of Vulnerability

*How happy are the poor in spirit, theirs is the
kingdom of heaven.*

—Mathew 5:3

That ultimately all the snakes are flowers, that God can be trusted to transform suffering and bring life from death is a wisdom
it takes a lifetime to grow into. We need to learn first hand that
failure can endow us with beauty and vulnerability can lead us
to love.

Some years ago when I went back to Trinity College for the
twenty-fifth reunion of our class, I was struck by how much we
had all been through in those years. Many still had the same
hair style and posture and kind of dress, but their faces, dear
and familiar, were marked by a kind of lined beauty of the
lived reality of suffering and love. A lot of storms and a lot of
mornings. Some very deep challenges to trust.

An image from that reunion has stayed with me ever since.
In one of the dorms where alumnae were staying there was a
power failure. I don't think we ever found out what caused the
sudden blackout, but when the people who were staying in
that dorm were trying to shower and get dressed for the luncheon, the electricity suddenly went off.

I was seated next to someone at the meal who had been a
great friend of mine. Marty (I will call her) and I were both

English majors. In our many shared classes we had gotten to know each other well.

Those in our class would all remember how stunning Marty was with a marvelous sense of her own style. She took trouble with how she looked, and even used to sleep on giant pink rollers, those terrible torturous devices which women used to set their hair in those days. She had shoulder length, shining blonde hair which would catch your eye across the college auditorium at assemblies. I would see guys notice it across the room at a social.

As I sat next to Marty at lunch at the reunion I heard her telling the story of the power failure in their dorm, laughing about how she couldn't iron the dress she had taken out of her suitcase, or blow-dry her hair or use a curling iron. (The days of the pink rollers were long gone.) The blue silk dress she wore still had suitcase folds across it, her hair was just kind of hanging down.

"That's just how it is, Hick," she said, laughing, calling me by the nickname she alone used to call me, short for my maiden name of Hickman.

That's just how it is for all of us, I thought. We've all been through it. Power we once counted on was shut off. Marty had learned this lesson tragically: her dazzlingly successful husband, whom we all knew from their dramatic courtship, had deserted her with no warning, emptying every account, leaving her with their three little boys. She never heard from him again.

The failure of something central in life leaves us exposed to one another in our struggling humanness, rumpled, unfixed-up, vulnerable, real. And what I realized looking at Marty, seeing her lovely face, softened and seasoned, was that it can leave us more endearing still. That realization has grown deeper in me through the years. I have come to grasp the truth that vulnerability can be a doorway to love.

I had a powerful experience of this on my fiftieth birthday. My closest friends from the little town where I had raised my kids had planned for a long time to take me to the big city a hundred miles away for an elegant lunch, an exchange of stories, and shopping for a birthday dress.

What we did not plan was that in the morning just before they were to pick me up, I got terrible news. Chaotic news. The kind of news that makes you feel as if the breath has literally been knocked out of you. It was the worst possible report from a doctor about someone in my family I love with all my heart.

When my friends came to the door they knew something was very wrong. I told them, briefly, what I had just heard, and walked to the car with them in a kind of daze. I think I said almost nothing on the hundred mile drive.

I will never forget how they were with me that day, these wonderful women who have shared their lives with me the past twenty-five years. If I wanted to talk, fine; if I didn't, fine. If I wanted to eat, fine; if I could only push the birthday cake around my plate, that was fine, too. All they were insistent on was that I was not going to spend my fiftieth birthday alone.

It was late afternoon when we went into a department store, our favorite through the years. It was one where we had shopped together for a lot of special occasions, for something to wear for a child's graduation, for an interview for a job, or for the role of mother of the groom. And now, today, for a dress for my fiftieth birthday. I hadn't much heart for looking, but it seemed important to us all to do it anyway. A kind of trusting in life, a claiming of the truth that pain is not all there is.

We looked and looked and found nothing. It was a strange year for styles, skirts very short and straight, colors kind of muddied, fabrics brittle and impractical. Finally we found a dress unlike any of the others, a throwback almost, to a material and style that might have been in fashion when we were in school. It was red plaid with a white collar and cuffs on the short sleeves. It had a wide belt of the same plaid, and pearl buttons all the way down the front. It was long, almost ankle length. I tried it on, and it fit me perfectly, becoming even to my strained face. My friends were delighted.

I began to protest. First of all, it was too expensive. Then, it wasn't really practical. Too long for work, too dressy for ordinary occasions, but not quite dressy enough for a big event. The plaid looked like fall, but the white collar and cuffs looked like summer. On many counts it was sort of neither one thing nor another. They silenced my objections with one voice: "We are getting this for you!!"

I brought it home in a bag with a red handle, and of all the dresses I have ever had it has become my favorite. Every time I look at it in my closet, it is as if my friends are there with me as they were that June day, celebrating my birth, and holding onto me through grief. Walking with me, breaking bread, drinking wine, telling stories, letting me know how much I matter to them. I have worn it again and again, on occasions of great importance. I wore it to the publisher's signing party for my first book. I wore it to the bridesmaids' luncheon for my son's bride. I wore it to my mother's wake.

It signifies for me the realization that vulnerability can be the doorway to love. On that day when dreadful news eclipsed candles and icing and ribbon and cards, I was utterly vulnerable. My friends, those four women who had come to mean so much to me, came right through the door of that vulnerability with love. Understated, sensitive, unmushy, patient, firm.

I thought about it for a long time afterward, thought about how much more I was able to experience their love because I was so broken open. I have noticed this dynamic over and over since then. I've decided that this is a key point of Christian revelation and the whole point of the Beatitudes. Why is it blessed to be poor? Being poor is terrible. It isn't the poverty that is blessed, it is that when we are poor, when we are hungry, when we are mourning, we know we need love. Small kindnesses touch us deeply. Faithful companioning fills us with gratitude.

Something in me hastens to add honestly that vulnerability can be the doorway to other things as well. To mistreatment. To terror. To cynicism. Just as suffering does not always make us compassionate, vulnerability does not always lead to love. But it can. When we are vulnerable there is a heightened potential both to give and receive love.

I saw this in my father. He had Alzheimer's disease for the last ten years of his life, and he became more and more dependent. He had been a very powerful man, as I have mentioned, a general, the chief of his corps. He was tireless physically, and he was utterly responsible, helping everyone in his family, anyone in his charge, any friend who needed a hand. He was, until his late 70s, the strongest person in all of our worlds.

After he retired, it wasn't easy for Mom. She said, "Your father is used to moving a whole corps around the world and now I'm the only troop he has!"

And then came the disease that tangled the neurons of his brain. Slowly his power slipped away, first mental, then gradually physical. This man, who had been head of the Army legal corps, the Judge Advocate General of the Army, who had negotiated the final truce at Panmunjon in Korea, who had supervised the rewriting of the Uniform Code of Military Justice, who had met at least four presidents, Pope Pius XII, the Queen of England, General Chiang Kai-shek, at the end was reduced to powerlessness.

He began to need *us*. First his family, then, when we couldn't care for him ourselves any more, the wonderful people who were his caregivers. In those weeks and months and years, as he was forced to relinquish control over his life, as he became more and more vulnerable, he was opened up to receive. In that receiving he came into fuller being.

It is not something he would ever have chosen for himself. A blessing of Alzheimer's disease, we pointed out to each other over and over, is that the person does not realize with full consciousness how much they have failed. Because he wasn't completely aware of his condition he was able to let us help him without the burden of shame. He was able to let in our love.

Perhaps my favorite picture ever taken in our family is my son Randy by Dad's bedside. During a break from school in the final summer of Dad's life, Randy went to Tennessee to help take care of him, feeding, changing, bathing, encouraging, talking with him. It was very important to Randy to come.

Years before, when Randy was in the sixth grade, he ran through our sliding glass door that he assumed was open, and needed hundreds of stitches for the injuries. My father immediately flew East from San Diego on the "red-eye special," and was there when Randy woke up in the morning. He stayed with us until Randy's stitches came out, and he was OK again. Randy never forgot that loving support, and he was honored that Dad now needed him.

The picture shows Dad, no longer able to walk, lying in bed, looking up at Randy. Randy is looking out at the camera, the same bone structure as Dad's showing in his face, the same strong nose and generous mouth. Randy is muscled and brown, holding Dad's pale hand in his. Dad is focused on Randy with an expression of pride and wonder, delighting in the love and care of this strong, young grandson.

We get so afraid of chaos making us vulnerable. Of being needy, dependent, helpless. There can be grace hidden in powerlessness. If I were never hungry, I would be indifferent to food. If I never wept, I would not know the unspeakable gift of being comforted. If I were never vulnerable, I would miss walking through a doorway into love wearing a red plaid dress.

Part Two
What Helps Us Move to Creation

As we name the dynamic of chaos and creation, as we see blessing in struggle and find love in vulnerability, as we grow in hope in God's power to bring life out of what seems to be defeat and loss, we can sometimes come to a peace beyond understanding.

I am very grateful to say that I have had the experience of this peace. But this peace definitely comes and goes. When chaos starts cranking up again, I can will myself to trust and hope, but my feelings are of dread and terror all over again. That there is a mysterious order in the disorder, that chaos, instead of being the enemy, can actually be the source of unimagined life, can seem pretty abstract. The reality is that my stomach is in a great knot.

"Good grief, another rotten growth opportunity!" a friend cried as a series of crises rolled through her family like a stream of enemy tanks. "Where can I find a prayer for a shallow life?"

For the times of the knotted stomach, how do we make it through chaos?

How do we recognize the movement in us which is giving birth to hope even in the shadow of threat?

How do we embrace creation, opening ourselves to whatever beauty, goodness, freedom, and truth is offered to us?

How do we make room for gladness and safeguard our ability to laugh?

What helps? This is the question I would like to address in the rest of this book.

9

Holding on to a Core Belief

Anyone who lives in love lives in God.

—1 John 4:16

When storms of chaos gather over our world again, the first thing that can help is our core belief. In these moments we are thrown back on the convictions at the heart of whatever faith we have. These are times of significant testing, times when we find out if we believe in anything we can really hold on to.

As I have said in earlier chapters, what I have discovered in times of chaos is that my core belief is that we are not alone. God is with us. *How do we know this?* That is a very important question which certainly insists on being addressed in moments of great challenge.

Years ago, when Boo was a very little boy, he was afraid of the dark. He used to leave his bed and go climb in with Randy. Trying to reassure him one night, I went into his room and reminded him that God was with him. I remember his reply: "But I want to be with Randy, I can see him."

His protest pointed to the gulf between what we know with our senses and what we believe. It is the place of the great leap, the jump from the tangible— our big brother right across the hall—to what seems real to us in a different way.

How *do* we know God? Who or what is God to us? These questions are especially urgent in times of great struggle. Theologians call the process of answering those questions "doing theology." We all "do theology" by comparing what we have been taught about God by others with what we find to be true in our own lives.

Theologians say we put these two elements "in dialogue," comparing the scripture and teachings of a religious tradition with our own experience. In the process of letting these two sources "speak to each other," our personal convictions are formed. Each person does this in his or her own way, revising or confirming, rejecting or elaborating.

Life can throw light on scripture and tradition, and scripture and tradition can illuminate life. As a result of the exchange, as insights deepen or seem to contradict, each person is challenged to come to some personal conclusion about belief. These conclusions are what we are thrown back on in the midst of chaos.

What "doing theology" has produced in me over the years is the simple credo I have been expressing in this book. Just as theologians suggest, this credo is the result of an ongoing interplay between what I have learned about God from religious tradition and what I have learned about God from experience.

The Judeo-Christian scripture and tradition have taught me that there are two things God endlessly communicates to us:

I am with you.
The way I am with you is Love.

This is the core of the Hebrew scriptures (Old Testament), the story of the covenant of God with the Jews: "I will be your God, you shall be my people" (Leviticus 26:12). "My love for you will never leave you" (Isaiah 54:10). It is the essence of the Christian scriptures (New Testament), the story of Jesus. "God loved the world so much that he gave his only Son" (John 3:17).

In dialogue with my lived experience, the message in scripture of God's loving presence has been confirmed through the many stages of my life.

"How do you know God is present?" someone asked me in one of those incredible conversations that sometimes occur in airports. The exchange had begun when he had inquired about what I was travelling to do, and I had answered "To give a retreat to Air Force chaplains." This led to the topic of God, and to his question, crucial to all of us, of how God's presence can be known.

My answer to him and my fundamental experience is that the most consistent confirmation of God's presence in my life has been through relationships, through experiences of love.

In the powerful music from the French monastery in Taize (to which countless people, more young than old, make pilgrimage each year) there is a setting for the ancient Latin refrain: *Ubi caritas et amor, deus ibi est.* This is the message of the First Epistle of John: "God is love. . . . Wherever love is there is God."

God can be experienced in the love other people show us and the love that comes to life in us for them. The deepest energies inside of us are the stirrings of God-life. We are moved by the Spirit into our hunger to love, to belong, to come home; into our yearnings and reachings, into our care and wonder.

An unforgettable line for most people who see *Les Miserables* is sung at the end of the play: "To love another person is to see the face of God." A theologian once said to me that it is equally true to say: "To love another person is to be the face of God." We know that God is with us through our moments of loving and being loved. This is particularly true of people whose love has been long and faithful in our lives.

I think of my sister Peggy, twenty months older than I am, who was waiting for me when I came home from the hospital as an infant, and who has been confidant and companion, challenger and cherisher ever since. She has never forgotten my birthday. She sends me flowers when I am heartbroken. She laughs at my jokes and gives me opinions on my clothes. We have been through a thousand family crises together, sometimes I am the front line, usually she is. When she is with me I feel as if, somehow, I will make it.

I think of my sister, Mary Lee, three years younger. She is the brightest, funniest, most creative of us: a poet, artist, sometimes a sculptor. She wrestles valiantly with mental illness, and there is no one in my life whose courage has been more a model when I am frightened, or whose generosity is more an inspiration. What she has, she shares. As simple as that. She remembers so many stories of our childhood, obscure events, nonsense rhymes that Dad made up, names we called each other. She reminds me of them, chuckling, recreating the long history of our love.

We can know God's presence through our own families, or through those who are like loving family to us. We also know it through our friends, sometimes through their just being with us as we deal with something hard.

For seven years, as I have mentioned, I helped run a sabbatical program, teaming up with the director, Gene Lauer. It was a very rewarding job, but it was also complex and demanding running those programs, morning, afternoon, many evenings. Working together, our friendship had grown deeper with each group, and our skill at collaboration more comfortable.

An incident happened one late summer, just as a new group was starting. I was at a turning point in my personal life, something potentially very painful, a loss, unexpected and cruel. I was to get some news, almost like a verdict or judgement, on the phone on Labor Day.

Gene knew the approximate time of the call. After an hour he began to call, but each time got a busy signal. We lived in the same apartment complex, and finally he came over and slipped a note under my door. It read "If when this is over, you want to talk, I would love to listen. If you don't want to talk, but would just like not to be alone, you are welcome to come over. I have made lamb stew and there is bread and wine. It will keep all evening. Feel invited, don't feel any pressure."

I was reeling from the blow of the phone call when I saw his note. I will never forget how that kindness felt. I walked over to his place. I remember the welcome, the taste of his stew, breaking the bread, drinking the wine. I remember telling him the story, pouring out as much of the heartbreak as I could form into words. I can still feel the particular totality of his acceptance.

When I think of the presence of God revealed in moments of friendship, I also think of my great friend, Benni. She has been my friend so long, that if someone asks how long, after she says "Thirty years," she adds, "Of course, we met as newborns in the nursery." One incident will illustrate how she has communicated God's love.

The day before I was leaving for what would amount to a three-day social event, my watch, which I had gotten for high school graduation, broke. It was the only watch I had. I stopped by Benni's that afternoon and I told her I was worried about getting to all these complicated events on time without a watch. She said: "My husband gave me a new watch for Christmas, why don't you take it? I only wear it when I'm dressed up."

It was a beautiful watch, delicate in gold with real diamonds. "Are you sure?" I asked. I had never worn a watch like that. "Of course," she said.

I put it on carefully, and on the way home I stopped at another friend of ours to drop off a baseball glove one of her sons had left in my car. When I came in her kitchen door she spotted the watch. "Isn't that Benni's new watch?" I explained to her that mine had broken and that Benni had lent this one to me.

"You can't take that watch! It is very valuable. Her husband gave it to her for Christmas. What if you lost it? What if you broke it? What if you forgot and wore it into the shower?"

I realized she was right and drove back to Benni's, knocked and walked in to where she was in the kitchen, taking off the watch as I walked. "I can't take your watch. What if I lost it? What if I dropped it and it broke? What if I forgot and wore it in the shower?"

I was in the process of handing it to her when she said: "You don't understand, do you?"

"What?"

"You're worth it!" she said as she handed me back the watch.

I smile every time I think back on that afternoon in her kitchen. It is symbolic for me of the unspeakable gift of having friends and family who tell us, in so many ways, that we are worthwhile, who wait for us when we are reeling from heartbreak, who confirm for us our core belief that we are not alone. When we are with each other on the journey we show each other the face of God.

10

Remembering That God Initiates

Aslan is on the move!

–C. S. Lewis

That God is with us, a presence of love, is the core of the religious tradition in which I have been formed. It is the core experience of my own life. There have been moments of great power and luminosity, there have been other moments of subtle tenderness. However, these moments do not always come when I am looking for them.

A very important realization for me has been that even though God is always with me, there are times when I lose my sense of God's presence. There are times when I am thrown back to my core belief and wonder if I have somehow just made it all up. There are times when the best prayer echoes the father praying for the healing of his son in the gospel: "I do have faith. Help the little faith I have!" (Mark 9:25).

One of the finer aspects of having lived for several decades is that I've had a chance to discover that the times when God seems absent do not last indefinitely. I have also learned that it is not up to me to "fix" them. God initiates.

There was an incident long ago that has remained both an example and a metaphor for God's coming to me when I feel lost. It was the Sunday before Christmas 1963. We were visiting my husband's parents in the town where he grew up, and I woke up and got ready for the 7 a.m. Mass. I tiptoed out of the room we were sleeping in, trying not to wake the baby who had been up five different times during the night.

I pulled up in front of the church, and was very surprised not to see any other cars. It was the type of Florida winter morning when temperature inversion forms a heavy fog, shrouding familiar landmarks. There were no lights on at all in the church. Where is everyone? I wondered. I had been coming to church here every time we visited, always to this early Mass. That there were no lights and no cars, the fog moving dankly around everything I could see, gave me a chilling Twilight-Zone feeling.

Off balance in the strangeness of the setting, I suddenly felt the disorientation that was the current state of my whole life. I was twenty-one with a six-week-old baby, my body still healing from childbirth, heavy with nursing, clumsy from lack of sleep in night after night of colic crying.

Confused by the vast difference between my romanticized anticipation and the unremitting challenge of the reality of motherhood, I felt overwhelmed by the enormity of responsibility for this tender, demanding, exquisite, consuming, little life. I was outwardly adult, but inside bewildered and lost. I sat in the car in the dark for what seemed like a long time.

And then, out of the fog, there came a tall figure, striding along in a black raincoat, a Sunday paper stuck in the crook of his arm. He came right to my Volkswagen and opened the passenger side door. "Ah, little one," he said in a County Kerry brogue, "Ye came for Mass, did ye? Ye haven't haird that I've come and changed everything. Go home now. Come back at eight-tharty. I'll be lookin' for ye."

I went home and came back. In vestments instead of a raincoat, the priest walked out of the sacristy, looked around the whole church until he saw me and grinned. Then he turned to the altar and began.

Through the years I have often thought of that morning, of sitting in my car in front of a church with no lights on, the fog closing in, lost-ness taking me over. And how, out of the swirling central Florida mist, there strode an Irishman. From that time on, in the many rounds with loss, the many bouts of letting go that life is built around, God sometimes seems to come to me and say: "Ah, Little One."

That story is a good reminder for me that the divine presence is a dynamic presence, not some stone idol to be carried around, but an active presence. God communicates: "I am with you always, saving you, setting you free, bringing you home, calling life from death." Finding you in the fog.

That God *initiates* is a vitally important truth which can easily be forgotten. It helps me in the times of the knotted stomach. I try to remember that connecting with God is not all up to me. I can lose sight of it in times I have come to think of as February.

During my first winter at Notre Dame, someone used the expression: "getting through February." For almost twenty years before I moved to South Bend, I had lived in central Florida. Winter in Indiana was, to understate it, very different. The first sub-zero weather stunned me. "What in the world *is* this?" I protested loudly. Any inch of skin exposed actually burned. My eyes ached alarmingly, like the fluid in them was actually turning to ice.

And it wasn't just cold that had people talking about "getting through February." It was the days without sun. It was the barrenness of branches and the absence of birdsong. It was the tediousness of struggling into mufflers and hats and mittens, into bulky stained coats and slush hardened boots, bracing to go into the wind.

February is much harder than the fall months because fall has festive elements like marching bands practicing for football games or trick-or-treaters in Frankenstein masks ringing doorbells to distract us from the cold. There is going home for Thanksgiving and getting ready for Christmas. But February.

February! One person said to me the reason there are only twenty-eight days is that no one could stand thirty or thirty-one. "It is a concrete proof of the existence of a merciful God," she said.

February in Indiana is a good metaphor for me for periods in my own inner life. Extended passages that are like a month on the calendar of my spirit. There sometimes comes a bleak stretch of long nights, of stripped trees, of frigid merciless wind that slices through coats and hope and steals warmth from any corner. They are times when God seems absent.

I have found that the only thing I can do during those times is to try to let go, to accept this time of absence and trust that God will sometime seem present again. I remind myself once more that it is not up to me. God will initiate.

The first time I began to comprehend this dynamic was about twenty-five years ago at the time of my divorce. It was my fiercest experience until then of a February in my soul. I had run completely out of warmth. I had come to the end of my endurance. The trees in my inner geography were all bare, the ground was frozen, I had nothing left to block the wind. I can remember plainly the image I had when I tried to pray. It was as if I were in a great stark frozen wood with my back against a tree, and I couldn't go another step. I found myself saying out loud: "I can't find you, God. You'll have to find me."

Only later did I realize how tellingly that statement expressed how I saw my relationship with God, my assumption that it was up to me to find God. How little I had grasped God's reaching for me. I thought somehow that *my* effort, *my* disposing myself, were the key to connection with God.

But I couldn't do it any more. There was no energy left inside me for anything. I was as lost as one can sometimes be in a whiteout when the snow blinds us totally, and we can't tell the road from the precipice. Perhaps this is one of the reasons for periods of God's seeming absence, for our "dark nights of the soul." We know with certainty that whatever happened to restore the light, it did not come from us.

All I can tell you is that God did find me in the days that followed. It was not dramatic or sudden. It was gradual and subtle, but deep. I had been reading the Narnia stories of C. S. Lewis to my children, and came across a wonderful passage in *The Lion, The Witch, and the Wardrobe*. For many years the witch has put a spell on the land so that it is always winter and never Christmas. Anyone who protests against the misery is turned to stone.

Then one day a new sound begins to be heard. At first the creatures can't understand it. What is this they are hearing? And then they realize: it is the sound of snow-melt. "Aslan is on the move!" they say. "Aslan is in the land." Aslan is the magnificent lion-Christ figure of the Narnia tales.

Twenty-five years ago, in that February within my being, my back to a tree in a frozen wood, I began to hear the sound of snow-melt. There was a warming. A freshening. A quickening. Aslan was on the move. God was coming to me. I noticed myself noticing things. One of the kids, for the first time since birth, hung up a wet bath towel. There were tomatoes at the fruit stand. Doing dishes after supper I remembered something funny and started to laugh. It was something my neighbor said, I think, maybe one of her comments like "Honey, I'm so old I was around when the Dead Sea was still sick." Waking in the morning I realized that I looked forward to the day.

I have found in the many years since then that after times when God seems absent, God makes God's presence known again. When my mother died, a dear friend of mine, Arthel Cline, wrote to me, alerting me to be on the lookout for God's presence.

Her letter said, "I hope this loss of your mother is a signal to be the wonderful nurturing mother to yourself who reminds you (as medieval mystic Meister Eckhart wrote): 'Be prepared at all times for the Gift of God. And be ready always for new ones! For God is a thousand times more ready to give than we are to receive!'" Arthel's letter really helped me be open to the gifts, the out-reachings of God. There were a lot of them.

Two weeks after Mom died I gave the keynote address to the annual gathering of the National Council of Catholic Women. I was almost haggard with the strain of the summer, and I was working on my talk on the plane coming to Chicago. The weeks I had expected to have to work on it had been spent by Mom's hospital bedside or making the fourteen hour drive back and forth to where she was.

When I got off the plane to do the keynote I was stiff and sore and tense. Waiting at the end of the jetway I saw a young man with a cardboard sign with my name on it. He had been sent by the conference committee to meet me. He walked me out the O'Hare lower level door to a stretch limousine! I had not only never ridden in one, I never knew anyone who had ridden in one.

I wish I had a picture of the driver's face when he put my bag in the trunk, that huge carpeted trunk built for bags of leather and tapestry with combination locks in polished brass. My battered, stained, red carry-on that I had gotten for $24.95 at Service Merchandise thirteen years before looked strange in that fancy trunk.

I gave him my best smile to reduce his embarrassment and got in the back seat. Back seat is hardly the word! I have lived in rooms that were smaller than that back seat. It was my *compartment*. Velvet and wood, music and refreshments, windows I could see out of but others could not see into. They probably thought I was someone elegant and famous. We took off from the curb and I started to laugh. Arthel had said God would be on the move. This was definitely *on the move*!

The council's gathering was a wonderful group, women from all over the country, many of them more of Mom's generation than mine, enthusiastic about this national convention. I spoke to them about hope. I told them about the stretch limousine. I asked them about God's initiating love in their lives, and they responded with a standing ovation.

The reachings-out of God are seldom so dramatic. They may be a star seen through a cloud or a letter that we want to save. They may be small exchanges of humor like one that hap-pened to me one night in a grocery store.

I was in the frozen food section puzzling over the endless arrays of quick dinners. I was cranky and tired and cynically reminding myself that they all taste exactly like the box they were frozen in. I overheard an elderly couple talking nearby. "You know it's strange, isn't it, Robert," she was saying, "the less these dinners have in them, the more they cost. If they have no cholesterol, no salt, no calories they are the most expensive." "Don't forget the extra charge for no taste!" I said, and we all laughed.

Getting through February, in Indiana or in our souls, is not up to us.

The God who seems absent will come to us again. It is an enormous comfort to me to have discovered that, in some way I may not expect, God will initiate, breaking into chaos with blessing.

II

Caring for Ourselves and Others

*Jesus said, "You must love the Lord your God
with all your heart, with all your soul, and with
all your mind. This is the greatest and first commandment. The second resembles it: You must
love your neighbor as yourself."*

—Mathew 22:37-39

In times of chaos we are helped by what we believe. In addition to what we believe, we can be helped by what we *do*.

It fascinates me to hear the things other people do that help
them. I have had extraordinary conversations with people
about this—friends, family, colleagues, strangers. I am always
trying to learn more about what helps. In this and the following chapters I will share ten things that can be effective for me.

The first thing I think strengthens us in times of great stress
is conscious, intentional caring. Loving ourselves, loving others,
and expressing that love in acts of caring. A core belief that we
are loved by God fuels and sustains our ability to love. Love is
the *energy* of creation.

Years ago I was introduced to the importance of loving
myself by a priest. It was a very hard time in my life. The world
as I had known it had fallen apart with the divorce. I had

sought out the priest, a Jesuit I knew and respected, for some kind of spiritual direction in the midst of my disorientation and confusion.

"I am going to send you on a mission, Pat," he said.

"Oh dear," I said to myself, bracing for what he would say next. "I'll have to take the kids out of school, get shots, learn a new language." (I had such trust for this good man that I probably would have at least considered going to a remote area of another continent if he thought it was what I should do.)

Then he continued: "The mission is this: Go to yourself."

"Here's what I want you to do. Go to a good store and buy some special soap with delicate fragrance and a pretty shape. Then buy a lovely hand towel with embroidery or lace, and some fine lotion. Every day for the next month, I want you to take care of your hands. Wash them tenderly and dry them gently, and smooth the lotion into them several times a day. And each time you do, let yourself feel how much God loves you."

He went on: "The mission we are sent on at birth, more than anything, is that we are entrusted with ourselves. God called you by name before the Daystar, ancient scripture tells us. When you die, God will not ask you, 'What did you accomplish?' or 'How perfect did you become?' But God will say, 'How did you care for my friend? How did you keep her warm, make her laugh, challenge her to grow? Tell me all the stories about the way you cared for my beloved one.'"

When I left his office I drove straight to a good department store and bought soap and towels and lotion. I still have the towels: blue and white gingham trimmed with ribbon and white eyelet lace. In the midst of chaos over the years I have used them, continuing the fundamental mission "Go to yourself."

Conscious caring for ourselves in a way that connects us to God's tender care for us is something that can help when our world has fallen apart or some portion of it has been turned upside down. It isn't always easy to do.

I find that what directs me best toward myself when I'm upset or frightened is real empathic listening from a friend. I am rich in friends who give me listening. Kathleen, for instance, lives far away, but we make dates on a regular basis to catch up on our lives by phone. We set apart a block of time for a visit, pouring coffee or a glass of wine on each end. The last time we talked I was in a highly frustrated state, irritable and jumpy, fuming at an infuriating let-down from someone I was working with.

"Isn't that the pits?" Kathleen said, "You not only have to deal with the disappointment, but with the toll all that stress takes on your mind and body. It's like for a while you can't enjoy being inside your own skin!"

"Exactly!" I exclaimed, suddenly feeling better because she had put into words what my crabby mood and squirmy body were expressing. Her listening really freed me to feel closer to myself.

Along with caring for ourselves is conscious caring for others. I put the caring for ourselves first because I believe we are far better able to love others if we truly love ourselves.

It has been important for me to understand why the commandment "Love your neighbor" includes "as yourself." To give to others freely, to spend myself for others without losing myself, I need a clear sense of my own worth. I need to attend to myself with real reverence.

But just caring for myself without opening up to give myself to others can be a road that leads nowhere. Pain can be very isolating. Turning in on myself exclusively is dangerous. Not only may I stagnate, but I might miss the abundance that comes in the interaction of giving and receiving.

Focusing on the concerns, needs, and suffering of others can move me out of my own morass. Reaching inside myself for what I might be able to offer gives me a chance to be a partner in creation.

I have seen the wonder of this on the faces of little kids when they did something nice for someone. Recently my grandson Jacob picked flowers for his mom on a day she wasn't feeling well. When I came to visit a week later he proudly led me to the flowers, long past their prime but still in a vase in the middle of the table. "I picked these for Mommy and made her feel better!" There are stars in the Milky Way that do not shine as brightly as his eyes did at that moment.

I have heard many stories from college students who discovered the power of helping others. "I was so homesick I thought I would have to drop out," one young woman said to me. "But I saw the notice that we could go for an hour and read to the blind . . . or serve food in the soup kitchen downtown. I began to volunteer three times a week, and it took my mind off my own loneliness."

Many students and adults who take part in building houses with Habitat for Humanity say the experience gives them a whole new perspective on their lives. They see their troubles in a new way. They understand differently their place in the human family.

Our experiences of suffering can close us in on ourselves. Sometimes the pain is so great that we can do little but huddle and grieve. We need to lament. But if we can gather the strength to reach out as well as reaching in, significant things happen. We can make a difference in the lives of others, and they make a difference in ours.

We begin to see that our time and care and resources can relieve immediate needs, that our work for societal change can contribute to altering the pattern of need in the world.

We see how our experiences of suffering can open a compassionate bridge to the lives of others. If we have had times when we ourselves have felt powerless we can empathize with so many who have no protection against violence, those to whom the world seems indifferent. When our lives are disrupted by some kind of conflict, we may see more clearly what life is like for those who live with war. When we have physical suffering, we may think differently of countless millions for whom pain, with little medical relief, is the daily context for their lives. An invaluable gift of insight and compassion can be given to us.

It is empowering to learn that we have something to offer precisely because we have some understanding of difficulty. This is the basis for the effectiveness of support groups. People help others who are in similar life crises: those who have lost a child, are undergoing cancer treatment, are mentally ill, are dealing with divorce. It is the basis for the singular success of Alcoholics Anonymous.

What it all comes down to for me is what has been one of the most significant creations from my chaos, an unshakeable and fundamental awareness that *we are all in this together.*

When I reach out I am enhanced by the experience that what I have to offer is of value to another. But in addition to my being able to contribute, there is a very profound return gift. If I am allowed to offer care to another, to enter the country of their chaos, I can be touched by their courage. I can feel in the deepest part of me the solidarity and mutuality of the human condition.

Through the years I have known many people who have worked in ministry of some kind in other cultures. Each one of them has described what they call "reverse evangelization." This means that they left the U.S. with the idea that they were going to bring something to the people they would serve: truth, caring, physical necessities.

Over and over again they would say that they received as much or more than they gave. My friend, Tom Smith, who has worked for years with people living in poverty in Africa, has tears in his eyes sometimes when he speaks of how he is constantly touched by the love of the people, by the incredible bravery with which they live their difficult lives, by their joy in celebration, by their enduring hope despite so much deprivation and sorrow. What most often happens when we reach out is anything but one-sided. It is an exchange of grace.

This grace came to me when I spent a week at the University of Florida hospital with my friend Lona. She

81

received an alarming test result after a routine examination, and a follow-up sonogram indicated a tumor on her ovary. Because she had contracted breast cancer five years before, and because her mother died of ovarian cancer, her doctor was very concerned. Surgery was scheduled as soon as possible.

My friend Benni and I insisted on going with her, and the three of us drove to Orlando to pick up Lona's sister, Linda, who flew in from Connecticut. The next day we made the three hour trip to Gainesville. We were together for five days.

Joining Lona in this moment at the edge of the unknown, poised over the abyss between life and death, is something I will not forget. I look back with great gratitude that I was able to be part of it, to experience her gutsiness, her sense of humor, her humble opening of herself to Mystery.

She insisted that we all go out to dinner the night before her surgery, even though she could only have clear liquids. She chose a fine Chinese restaurant nearby. When the elegant waiter asked for her order she grinned and said "I will have the won ton soup without the wons or the tons." She sipped tea when her soup was finished, delighted that we were enjoying our meals. There was no way she would miss the party!

Of course there were moments when she was anxious, in pain, even cranky. But she let us share that too. We were together in the chaos.

The surgery had the best possible outcome: it turned out she had a strangulated fibroid tumor that had become infected. There were absolutely no signs of cancer! We all wept and prayed with other family members who had driven up that morning, our arms around each other.

A week later flowers were delivered to me. The card said: "What incredible friends I have! Thank you."

What I have tried to tell Lona, and I'm not sure she completely understood it, was what it did for me to be there. It wasn't just about the outcome, although I still get lightheaded with relief when I look back on it. It was the depth at which we were together. It was being trusted to see the fear and the bravery with which she faced the trial: whether it would be good news or bad, deliverance or death, I was invited to walk with her and Benni and Linda in the Mystery.

It reminded me of Boo and Caroline after their son Hunter was born. The labor had been dreadful, prolonged many hours more than it need have been. They were on an Army post where there were lots of child-bearing couples. It was a night of full moon, and there were five women having babies and only one doctor.

Boo and Caroline had gone to childbirth classes and he had trained to be her coach. They went through the fifteen hours together minute by minute. He was helping her breathe, watching the monitors, encouraging her to push, anguishing at her wrenching pain that somehow didn't get the baby born; his muscles tightening, his breathing quickening with the sympathetic effort of the labor.

He ached to be able to do it for her for a while, relieve her pain, let her rest. It turned out the baby was very big—eight-and-a-half pounds—and Caroline is very small. The doctor needed to make an incision for the baby to push free. When at last he was born, the doctor said "A fine strong son," and put him in Boo's hands. "I just started crying," Boo said when he called to tell the news. "The floodgates opened. It all poured out." He brought the baby to Caroline and they held him together.

Two days later when my husband and I drove to Alabama to see them she was feeding the baby in the rocking chair. Boo led us over to them. My breath caught at the sight of the precious little person, Hunter Gordon, so new and red and beautiful, the perfect little hands and feet, the soft fair fuzz on the head still elongated from all those hours in the birth canal. "A thousand thousand welcomes," I whispered from endless generations of our Gaelic past.

But at the same time I saw the baby, I saw the arresting exhaustion on the faces of those grown children I so love. Boo and Caroline were gray with prolonged lack of sleep, but lit with something more. Their eyes, still wide with trauma, had a knowing. There was a different texture to their bonding. Through all those hours of chaos they had brought not only Hunter, but each other to a different place in life.

We are in this together.

Creation.

12

Connecting With Life

A single green sprouting thing would restore me. . . .

—Jane Kenyon

The first thing on my list of ten things that can help in the midst of struggle, in the times of the knotted stomach, is caring for ourselves and others. The second is surrounding ourselves with life. I had a startling experience of this not long ago—a bizarre example of an almost heroic attempt to do just this in the midst of chaos. It really made an impression on me.

My husband and I were driving home from Alabama after our visit to see the new baby when we stopped to see a cousin of his whom he had not seen for years. We had been given directions by phone to their place on the outskirts of a town. We turned at an ornate gate into what seemed at first glance to be a farm, and then at closer look to be almost an animal park.

When we stopped by the house and knocked on the front door we heard a screeching that stood our hair on end. Inside, in the living room, there were great birds on perches—more than a dozen enormous parrots, bright blue, red, chartreuse, white—huge birds with beaks that could clip a bunch of thirty bananas from a tree without losing a beat in flight—all of them screaming in high pitched squawking shrieks that were actually painful to the ears.

The birds were only the beginning. The cousins took us on a tour of the property. There were deer and horses and a Jerusalem donkey they had brought back from Israel. There were peacocks, both brightly colored and albino. There were six black swans. There was an insistent goose who stalked us for ten minutes, gabbling, outraged, ordering us out of her part of the yard. There was a large pond with fish of all kinds. A thirty pound catfish, we were told, lived in the waters. Following us on the outing was a *white wolf*!

I was utterly, completely overwhelmed. By the time we left I was in a daze. What could this mean? Why would anyone choose to do this? Why would you live with this noise and confusion? All these animals to feed and be concerned for? It was clearly quite deliberate and done with great joy.

My husband had explained before we arrived that his cousin has Crohn's disease, a slow, debilitating illness in which the intestines can be progressively destroyed by stress. He had undergone all the surgery he would be able to stand. Why, I asked myself, when you are weaker and weaker and in more and more distress, would you surround yourself with these animals, with such cacophony, so many demanding needs to be met?

And then suddenly I saw the meaning. As he and his wife and family dealt helplessly with the probable encroachment of his death, they were surrounding themselves with life. Excessive, rampant life. There was a deafening screeching at impending fear, the air filled with the sound of wings and the cries carried on the wind: the howl of a wolf and the braying of a donkey, the argumentative squawk of a goose. Huge fish, leaping and splashing. *"Le' chayim!* To life!" they were shouting in the face of death.

Life all around us can bolster us in chaos. For most of us this would mean something simpler than our cousin's amazing menagerie. It might be an Irish setter or a calico cat. It might be a tree outside a window that we can watch through the seasons. It might be learning the names of stars or keeping track of the phases of the moon.

In this era of my life I am incredibly graced to live in an apartment that looks right out on Tampa Bay. The play of the light on the water is endlessly varied and beautiful. While I am looking out I know that I am the only one who can see this exact angle, this precise view of color and shape, this intersection of sea and sky. I think of God as creating this glimpse just for me.

Early in the morning I look for dolphins. Sometimes weeks will go by and I cannot spot one, and then while I am watching the pelicans dive or the sea gulls skim, suddenly there is a splash that I know a bird did not make, and then a fin, then the curve of a back breaking the surface, then the leap—a dolphin. Each time it moves me deeply.

We also sometimes see small green parrots, descendants of birds that were brought in cages, I am told, who escaped to find this a perfect climate and thrive in the wild. They fly in bunches, six or ten, with great energy and chattering, a cloud of merriment and color coming past the window. Sometimes when feeling in great need of comfort I have seen dolphins and parrots on the same morning.

For the times of the knotted stomach, it helps to connect with life; to open the door of our chaos to the creation around us. It pulls us out of our isolation, it distracts us from dismal concern.

The most powerful manifestation of creation for me these days is my grandchildren, these five little boys born within three years. I finally understand now something I have found amusing for years—grandmothers carrying around actual *albums* of pictures of their grandchildren. You want to carry pictures because words can't do justice to the wonder you feel about them.

Of course, pictures don't communicate it, either. Other people can't see what you see: can't see the exquisite new beauty born of the life you gave birth to long ago; can't see the expressions, the responses, the growing and flowering that are both so familiar to you and so fresh; can't feel the miracle that your child somehow grew up, safely and uniquely, and gave life on to this one. Others can't appreciate that the life that was passed on to you, you passed on; and that life is now being passed on all over again. They can't see that you are looking at the living story of your family. The story of the human family from the beginning of time.

I look at these boys, their beautiful little faces and perfect rounded little bodies, I hear the husky, musical little voices, I watch the hilarious and important little activities, and I just well up with the enormity of the grace of it all.

Sometimes I have an ache in the back of my throat with the intensity of my love for them. And the fact that they love me back literally takes my breath away. I get overcome with a tidal wave of tenderness when they run to me calling "Grandmaaaa, Grandmaaaa," or put their arms around my neck in an unexpected hug, or bring something they treasure to show me, or fall asleep in my lap.

I think I cherish these moments especially because I know they are totally honest. They aren't old enough to do it to please their parents or because they know Christmas is coming. They just do it because they have real joy in seeing you. *They* have joy in seeing *me*! *They*, for whom my heart almost stops with wonder, they love me too. Well! It is quite the most amazing experience.

When chaos comes stalking me these days, I think about the little ones, connecting with life.

13

Reading and Remembering

Could you read a Sustaining Book, such as would help and comfort a Wedged Bear in Great Distress?

—A. A. Milne

Creation breaks through to us when we are surrounded with life.

This can be meadows or menageries, galaxies or grandchildren, the sunset or the sea.

After I wrote "connecting with life" on my list of what brings strength in chaos, I added two things, one after the other: reading and remembering. Books tell the stories of how people in time or imagination have dealt with difficulty. When I read I often remember breakthrough moments of my own.

Books are great sources of comfort for me, especially old, familiar, beloved books. When I am distressed I turn to favorites, to Ray Bradbury's *Dandelion Wine* or Oscar Wilde's fairy tales or *The River* by Rumer Godden. Sometimes I read plays aloud to myself, like *Shadowlands* about C. S. Lewis or *A Man for All Seasons* about Thomas More.

It seems as if the more I read old books, nearly knowing them by heart, the words begin to have a life bigger than the page. Parts of the A. A. Milne's *Winnie-the-Pooh* books are like that for me. The love in those books is so simple and real.

I especially prize the passage I rediscovered when what I am calling chaos was significantly on the move in my life, a crisis I needed to deal with in every generation of our family. It was a Truly Dreadful Time (Milne capitalizes important words) quite the equal of the time when Pooh Bear got stuck in the exit of Rabbit's hole after eating too much honey. Perhaps you remember that he was stuck for quite a while and made this request of Piglet: "Could you read a Sustaining Book, such as would help and comfort a Wedged Bear in Great Distress?"

In my crisis time I felt Wedged in Great Distress and I found it quite sustaining to read the section in *The House on Pooh Corner* about the Blustery Day, just four little paragraphs after the description of the very strong wind blowing.

> *"Good-bye," said Eeyore [the donkey]. "Mind you don't get blown away little Piglet. You'd be missed. People would say: 'Where's little Piglet been blown to?' really wanting to know."*
>
> *In the Hundred Acre Wood Pooh and Piglet listened nervously to the roaring gale in the tree tops.*
>
> *"Supposing a tree fell down, Pooh, when we were underneath it?"*
>
> *"Supposing it didn't," said Pooh, after careful thought.*
> *Piglet was comforted by this.*

I was comforted too.

That passage reminds me of something that reduces my anxiety in chaos. I think of times in the past that I feared the worst, and the worst did not happen. The tree did not fall down while I was underneath it.

There is one instance I think of nearly every time I am really worried about something. It happened twenty-five years ago. Boo, who was about three, had gone out on a bike ride, riding on the seat behind his dad. Our Dalmatian, Max, was running along beside them.

At one point on their route they went through some scrub vegetation on the path, and a large rattlesnake struck from the brush, biting Max. It was spring, the time snakes shed their skins. For a few days before the new skin grows back snakes are almost blind. They have no eyelids. All movement irritates them and they strike at almost anything. By great fortune Max was running right beside Boo. If the snake had not bitten Max it would have struck Boo's little bare leg below his red shorts.

Somehow Jimmy got Max and Boo back to the house and asked me to start for the veterinarian's office while he tried to locate him on the phone and ask him to meet me there. All the way to the office Max was thrashing around, actually throwing himself back and forth over the seat of the station wagon, making harsh noises of pain. The doctor was there waiting when I pulled up.

He quickly anesthetized the dog's leg with a shot, then shaved the area of the bite and cut an X into it, just like I'd always heard was the thing to do in the treatment of snake bite. He then pulled over a hose from a sink faucet which was supposed to be on a reverse setting so there would be suction to pull out the venom. For some reason the hose setting was wrong, and, instead of providing suction, water sprayed out all over the office.

The doctor swore loudly, grabbing for the faucet to switch the lever. He then handed me the hose and told me to suction the wound while he scrambled to mop up his equipment and papers all over the room.

"Hold it," I said. "I have no idea how to suction this wound. You are the doctor. What I do know how to do is clean up mess. I have years of practice. I'll mop up, you treat the dog." He laughed, and for the next ten minutes we worked side by side.

"Well," he said finally, "that's all we can do. We'll just have to see how he is in a few hours. I'm going to keep him here and check on him. Call in the morning and we'll let you know."

"What are his chances?" I asked.

"I'd say fifty/fifty," he replied. "It was a very big snake. It all depends on whether it had struck anything else in the last day or so. That would determine how much venom it had left when it bit Max."

I remember sleeping very little that night, and watching the clock inch toward 7:30 when I could call. At 7:25 the kids and I went to the kitchen phone. Just as I was reaching to dial I heard a peacock scream from down the street. Our friends, the Fosters, kept peacocks by their barn. A cold chill went all the way through me. I had read in books that the peacock screams to signal death.

I called the vet's and Moses Smith, the wonderful African American man who assisted the doctor, answered the phone. "Moses, it's Pat Livingston. I'm calling about Max."

"Max . . . Max . . . that . . . got . . . bit . . . by . . . that . . . big . . . old . . . snake?" (Moses talks very, very slowly.) "Well now Max. He's . . . (there was a long pause, in which I felt sure he was trying to think of the gentlest way to tell me he was gone) Max . . . he's here with me almost wagging his tail clean off."

I was so weak with relief I sat down on the kitchen floor. When the kids saw me they cheered.

I've never forgotten that. I say to myself: "Do not be terrified of ominous portents. The peacock scream was not a predictor of disaster." Max lived many long years after that, and his descendants are still wagging their tails in family kitchens.

Retelling that story is an example of what my sister calls "the remembering trick." Reminding ourselves of times that we came through chaos well, times when a tree did not fall on us on in the Hundred Acre Wood. I remember, for example, when we got rid of the head lice with a stunning hair style, or when no operation was needed on the baby's skull, or when Lona's tumor was not cancer. When trouble looms, I tell myself the many times the snake bite wasn't fatal, and the peacock's scream portended healing and not death.

14

Laughing Amidst the Mess

Angels fly because they take themselves lightly.

—Jean Cocteau

In listing what can help us in times of chaos I next added two things I often think of together: mess and humor. They are connected for me because I find humor aids greatly in dealing with mess, and also because messy situations often teach us to laugh at ourselves.

A hard won insight about mess, which has proved valuable in subsequent moments of chaos, came to me when we were trying to make a home in our Tampa apartment. It was a saga so extreme that I finally understood that there must be something I was being encouraged to learn.

I have come to realize that when a situation drags on and on, or the same kind of thing happens to me over and over again, it is like a recurring dream. Something is trying to reveal itself. Something is on the move. This can be an invitation to discover something important.

Trying to get settled in our apartment was like a recurring bad dream. Each simple job took at least five times as long as expected. The first painter went bankrupt in the middle of the project. It was half-finished, on hold for weeks, until he finally admitted he was never coming back.

The next painter took over, but he painted the whole apartment the wrong color. Instead of white it was khaki, a kind of yellow brown. A beautiful job of painting, but a hideous color. His instructions had been to "match the existing paint," which was white. This should not have been too hard! It was not like working with a tiny paint chip from a chart. He himself could come up with no explanation for why he had painted it khaki. It took two coats and as many weeks to cover it with white.

The carpentry had similar stories. Shelves were built in the wrong place, the wrong doors were put on, furniture built for my office was too big to get through the doorway.

Appliances were sources of trouble. The water heater malfunctioned frighteningly. Pipes for the washer leaked after installation. The vent for the dryer disconnected in the ceiling.

The worst moment was when the new Murphy bed (a bed that folds up into a frame against the wall) pulled out of the wall and fell on the installer, a handsome, rather shy young man about twenty. I heard a loud noise and then his screaming in Spanish. I ran in, horrified. I was the only one home, and a wave of panic hit me when I realized it was up to me alone to drag the heavy queen-sized bed off of him. I'm still not sure how I got him free. His arm was dangling at a horrible angle. In the hospital across the street they set his arm in three places.

The point I am underlining is that each phase of the project was fraught with continual difficulty. It was seven whole months before we could unpack the boxes from the move. I had thought it would be a week or two. It never occurred to me to list every item in every box because I thought we would just unpack them after the moving truck left. Over the months, the frustration of needing something in one of the boxes, but having no idea where to begin to look, or having no energy to move fifteen boxes to get to it, was an everyday occurrence.

As weeks went into months with this endless frustration I felt myself sinking into chaos. I began to ask myself "What *is* it that I could be learning?"

Here's what I have concluded: I need to learn to be at home with the unfinished. Home is not about the perfect environment. It is about living in the loving presence of God and one another—in the middle of packing boxes, with khaki walls. There is an amazing verse in the gospel of John "Make your home in me as I made mine in you" (15:3). I remember how that affected me the first time I really understood it. The invitation to make God my home. And the stunning fact that God is at home in me. (This stirred up all kinds of images in me: God in a bathrobe. God in a rocking chair. God cracked up laughing. God drinking coffee. God taking a nap. God feeling safe, shutting the door against the craziness outside and saying: "Home at last!" God delighting in seeing me when I come in and asking me about my day.)

The chaos of trying to make a home in Tampa has challenged me to celebrate that God is home in me, and, in a deeper way than before, to make my home in God.

Being at home in the unfinished is a really wonderful grace. In a class on major world religions taught by my colleague, Gene Lauer, he described as a particular wisdom of Buddhism: "Don't strain to make things perfect. Life in the present order will never be perfect, so don't stretch to put everything right, to order all persons and things once and for all." A great resource in times of chaos, a comfort for the knotted stomach, is a friendly attitude toward mess.

Life is about living in the balance of the unbalanced, the imperfect, the never finished, never totally secure, never happily-ever-after. We have such a longing to have everything in order, under control, to have everyone we love healthy and safe. This is not a state that ever lasts. We have to learn to live with mess.

Nothing helps with this more than having a sense of humor. My friend Martha just told me this story: "I was expecting forty people for dinner last week when the sunken seating area in our living room began filling with water from the ground. More rain was predicted for the evening. My sister's suggestion was: 'Throw Japanese carp in there and call it live art!' Laughing helped me mop!"

To be able to laugh at the incongruous misfitting moments of daily life is an incomparable gift. And most of all to laugh at ourselves. We take ourselves so seriously. I was delighted earlier this summer by a gate agent in an airport who was making all his announcements in a way that poked fun at the solemn repetitive script of all boarding procedures.

For example, when it was time to begin he said with a perfectly straight face: "Please remain seated and passive and obedient until it is your turn. Avoid any form of milling and thrusting forward until your row is called. Then say 'Mother may I?'"

People were startled. They looked at each other in disbelief, putting down their papers, pausing in the act of dialing their cell phones.

He continued. "If there are any passengers who are not here, please check with the desk immediately." We began to laugh out loud. It was a trip that I had quite a bit of anxiety about, and as I laughed, I felt myself relax. I liked it that the airline could find itself funny.

People who know us well observe the laughable things about us. My friends who are good at fitness love to point out that I have almost an aversion to exercise. They say, "When Pat thinks about exercise she wants to lie down 'til the urge passes." When they tease me I quote a card I saw in a shop: "Working out is hard. All that stretching, bending and grunting. And that's just to get the leotards on."

Thinking of humor always reminds me of Mom. She had a wonderful wry sense of humor, but she was a terrible joke teller. She could never successfully complete a joke, always blowing the punch line. She loved it when we would tell jokes. Because of my work with people in ministry for twenty years I've heard a lot of religious jokes. I would pass them on to her.

One she really enjoyed I heard from Loughlan Sofield, a psychologist and a marvelous speaker. He tells of seeing a sign

on the lighted board outside a Methodist church that said:
"Sunday Morning Service Sermon: Jesus Walks on Water.
Sunday Evening Service Sermon: Searching for Jesus."

Mom really liked that, but every time she told it she would
begin with "Searching for Jesus," before she realized she had
ruined the joke. She had a goal to be able to successfully complete a joke some time in her life. The closest she came was
reading one, not risking trying to repeat it. She cut it out of a
magazine and read it to us:

> A little boy and his mom were walking in the
> evening while the sun was setting. "See the sunset
> God painted for us, Johnny?"
> "Yes! And he did it all with his left hand."
> "What do you mean?" his mom asked.
> "I heard them say in church today that Jesus
> is sitting on God's right hand."

This really struck Mom funny. She would get it out and
read it to us every once in a while, chuckling her rich chuckle.
The last time she ever was able to go to church was an Easter
Sunday. The second reading (Colossians 3:1-4) had this passage: "Set your heart on higher realms where Christ is seated
on God's right hand."

Mom poked both my sister Peggy and me at the same
time: "My joke!" she said in a triumphant whisper. On that
Easter day, when it had been such a struggle for her frail and
pain-filled body to come to church, her merriment was the
energy of creation.

15

Looking for Goodness

Knowing how to receive and remember goodness
is, in fact, the best way to prepare for trusting
when goodness seems absent.

—Demetrius Dumm, OSB

Reflecting on what helps us deal with chaos I have mentioned several things: a conscious caring for ourselves and others, surrounding ourselves with life, reading, remembering, learning to live with mess, laughing.

The next thing I want to describe is both a perspective and a practice. It has grown clearer and clearer to me in these last years how crucial it is to focus on goodness. I have been trying to do this in one way or another ever since I began to realize just how precarious a sense of gladness in life can be.

Quite some time ago when I was leaving on a dreaded trip a friend embarrassed yet greatly encouraged me by yelling down a jetway: "Livingston, look for the surprises!" That began my conscious awareness that we see what we are looking for. We can choose what we focus on.

I watched my friend Benni do this choosing. Her son was married right after Christmas last year. Ten days before the wedding her kitchen caught on fire! It not only burned up the stove and the cabinets, but it deposited greasy black soot everywhere in the house: all over the Christmas tree, all over the wedding presents. She had ten house guests coming for the festivities.

I will never forget her reaction. This was her actual response: "Hooray! This is the best excuse I have had in my life not to cook!!" She absolutely hates to cook, and not only was the Christmas baking ahead, but her houseguests would have been expecting regular meals to appear. "I am completely off the hook!!" she said. "Glorious day!"

That was ten days before. On the wedding day itself, records were set for rain in central Florida. Areas not far away were completely flooded out. There was a tornado watch posted all day. In fact, in the next county north, tornadoes hit and destroyed more than fifty homes.

Narrowly missing a tornado was not the only dramatic event of the wedding day. The bride's father tried on his rented tux and discovered that it did not fit him. In the late morning he took it to be altered to the store downtown that had rented the tuxes. He was in a dressing room having cuffs pinned when he heard a gruff man's voice say at the register: "Hand over all your cash or I'll shoot everyone in this store!"

The bride's father peeked through the curtain and saw a robber in a ski mask with a huge gun and found himself whispering to the tailor, "Give that man anything he wants. If he shoots me and doesn't kill me, I'll still get killed if I don't show up at the wedding!"

The robber ran out of the store with the money right into the arms of police! They had just happened to be driving by when the owner pressed a silent alarm under the counter by the register. When she was telling me the story at the wedding reception, Benni's eyes lit up with delight. "Close calls," she said, "and all of them in our favor! A wonderful start to their marriage."

Benni did not always have the knack of looking at the goodness in situations. She has worked on it long and hard. For years we have shared a practice I developed that I call "The One Good Thing." It is trying to build a habit of focusing on good things and telling about them. It involves having an agreement with friends and family that we will tell each other on a regular basis one moment that was graced for us, One Good Thing.

This is easy to do at dinnertime or at cocktail hour or with cookies and milk after school. It is helpful to link the telling of one good thing with a natural moment of gathering that is already in the rhythm of life.

Remembering goodness is a wonderful thing to do at bedtime. Sleep research shows that we get significantly more rapid-eye-movement (REM) sleep, the deep dream sleep that really restores and renews us, when we go to bed grateful. What may be more usual for many of us when we do not fall right to sleep is to worry, to think back on all the things we are concerned about. Going to sleep anxious *reduces* our REM sleep.

My great-aunt Caddie never heard of sleep research clinics, but she understood the principle. When she would say goodnight to us in the old family house on the Green River in Kentucky she would say, "Now if you can't go right to sleep, don't count sheep, honey, just count your blessings." It is the same idea.

Our example of One Good Thing doesn't have to be a big thing. The one that happened to me the day I was working on this chapter had to do with Novocain. I had gone to the dentist and had a very old filling replaced. There was not much of the tooth left and it needed lots and lots of drilling. It had taken four shots to numb my mouth, and I mean it was *numb*.

I had to stop at the grocery on the way home, and the checkout counter woman asked me a question. I tried to answer and bit my tongue. I couldn't feel the pain, but I knew it was really bad. I must have moaned, because she looked up startled. I mumbled to her that I had Novocain, and she said: "Oh no! Isn't that the most uncomfortable thing? Half your face is just dead. You smile and only half of you smiles. And you're afraid to speak because you will probably bite your tongue and you don't even know it until you taste the blood."

"Uh-huh!" I said, with so much feeling that she realized that is exactly what had just happened.

"I'm so sorry!" she said. Her eyes were the very sight of kindness, and she looked like she would have given me a hug if she had known me.

It's a little thing, maybe, kindness from a stranger. But when you have known unkindness, when you have had plenty of experience being discouraged and worried and lonely, it can be a gift. It can make a difference. In a difficult day it is certainly One Good Thing. It was a story to tell when my turn came.

I began to do this years ago with my younger sister, Mary Lee, when she was in the psychiatric ward of a hospital. As I mentioned, she has had an agonizing battle with mental illness, struggling with the terrible demons of her unbalanced brain for a very long time. This particular time she had had a total psychotic break and her husband finally decided to get a legal separation from her. She lost him, lost her two children, lost her home, lost them all at the same time. She was hospitalized for many months.

I used to call her every Thursday. It is an inexpressible helplessness to have someone you have loved all her life in that kind of torture. I would just try to listen with all my heart and be with her. She would pour, pour, pour out pain. I would be shaking when I hung up, and, after a while, I would be shaking when I dialed the phone the next time.

One day I was desperate at the end of the avalanche of anguish and I said, "I don't know if this sounds impossible, and if it is, just say so. But I wonder if you could look for even one good thing that happens during the week. I will, too, and we will tell each other when we talk."

She thought it was a good idea, and said she would start looking as soon as we hung up. "Like a treasure hunt in a garbage dump," was the way she put it.

There was never a week that she didn't have a story. Often there were several stories, of a roommate who got well enough to leave, of a visit from her daughter, of a tree that flowered outside her window, of sharing cigarettes with the other patients, of her son winning a Boy Scout badge, of a night when she had no bad dreams, of finally being able to paint again. Sometimes the One Good Thing was a joke. Her heavily medicated mind could not retain complicated jokes, but she did well with one or two line jokes, like: "Two men were talking. The first said, 'Hey Ralph, how is life treating you?' The second said, 'It isn't. I'm paying for every dang thing.'" She liked religious jokes, like: "How do they make holy water?" "Boil the hell out of it."

I began to look forward to our calls instead of being afraid of them. I would rejoice with her and she with me that there was goodness in our lives. We are still doing it. It has really made a difference.

A year ago I called her from a pay phone to the supervised living apartment where she now lives. She knew I had been terribly worried about my daughter-in-law Silvia who was past due in her second pregnancy. There were indications that the placenta was deteriorating. I had thought the doctor was going to take the baby the day before, but he did not. I was travelling on a speaking trip and kept calling for news.

As soon as I heard, I dialed my sister. I was shouting in the phone: "Get ready for this good thing: It's a boy! Eight pounds, twelve ounces. And he's fine! And Silvia is too! It all went well. And guess what. They named him after Dad!!"

"George?" she yelled back and I could hear that she was dancing around the room, "Really, they named him George?"

"Yes! George. His brother Jacob is already calling him 'George, George, George of the Jungle,' and he's only an hour old."

"Wahoo," she yelled, "George! All Riiiight! George! And how Dad must love it that now there are *five* boys. He was crazy about us, the three girls, but he would certainly get a kick out of five boys. . . . George! Well what do you know? *Yesssss.*"

Every time I think of that call I want to dance. She was such a great partner in my rejoicing. So much goodness to share.

I think that in these days that are especially challenging in our world and in our personal lives we need help in keeping our spirits up. One very simple thing is to pay attention to the good. It is hard, with the bombardment of bad news that comes at us from all the media, not to be overwhelmed with what is fearful and shocking and discouraging and sad. We can savor our moments of One Good Thing and pass on the tale of the experience to those we care about. A moment of beauty, a tender exchange, something that struck us funny.

I have noticed that my enjoyment is greatly deepened by the telling. There is an energy of excitement when the moment comes, a bit like unwrapping packages together. I have found that, because I know I am accountable for taking a turn with a story, I pay attention in a stronger way to life. My focus shifts from what went wrong to what went right.

This turns out to be a very important habit medically. I have been listening in the last few days to a tape of Deepak Chopra, the renowned medical doctor, teacher, and author who brings together the latest scientific insights of quantum physics and molecular biology with the ancient wisdom of India. He was talking about heart disease, and how studies show that the most significant factor in heart disease is not diet or exercise or even family history but one single thing: the person's perception that their lives are happy! Whether they see goodness in their lives.

Because I have been practicing this focus on goodness for a long time, it thrilled me recently to come across some splendid theology for why it is so important. It was a confirmation from an important source for what I already valued deeply.

The gift came from Demetrius Dumm, a scripture scholar and a dear friend. He linked goodness to trust. Demetrius is always speaking and writing about trust. He reflects on how inescapable sooner or later in life is the realization that human strength and autonomy are illusions. We are not in control. Life is disorderly. We are radically dependent on God.

I am indebted to him for his clear understanding, which I find very reassuring, that it is impossible to trust unless we have some experience of goodness. I think I always pictured trust as a sort of act of will. That trusting God was something I ought to be able to just make up my mind to do, and that it would somehow be a deficiency in me if I were afraid or overwhelmed. Dumm points out that trust has to begin in our sense of being deeply loved, a love that produces experiences of goodness.

How we deal in the present with some new threat is by counting on the goodness that we have known and experienced in the past. In his book *Cherish Christ Above All* Dumm writes: "Knowing how to receive and remember goodness is, in fact, the best way to prepare for trusting when goodness seems absent."

I think that is enormously profound and singularly practical. It is exactly what I have been trying to do through the years: *receive and remember goodness.* Let it in, savor it when it is happening. Then remember it: think about it as we go to sleep, write it in our journals, tell one another the stories. Pass on the good news.

I want to pass on a story of something that happened this fall. I was flying to Boise, Idaho, to do a retreat day for women. We were on the plane, everyone buckled up, when the pilot's voice came on. I knew right away it was not good news—there was that tense, frustrated sound that is very different from the tone of voice used in saying, "Thank you for flying Delta."

He informed us that the altimeter was not working. He said they were searching the airport for a spare, and if they could find one, it would only take about sixty seconds to replace. Thirty minutes later he came back on to say there were no spare altimeters for our plane in the airport, so we needed to find another way to get where we were going. Just pick up our luggage and go to the ticket counter.

I was two hours in the line. Right behind me was a young man from San Francisco who had been visiting his father. He was lean, maybe mid-thirties, with longish dark hair around a clean-shaven, kind face. He wore one gold earring. He had a pleasing voice, well spoken, and we had an easy off-and-on conversation standing there, not pressured or intense. From time to time he would make a gentle optimistic remark.

"This is going well," he said after an hour, looking at his watch, "only about five minutes per person." It startled me because it was the reverse of how I had been interpreting the same data silently to myself: "Good grief! This is taking at least five minutes for every single person! There are one hundred and fifty people in this line. We'll never get through."

Then a little later he said: "This is encouraging. Each person seems to be rebooked. No one has left furious. There are lots of options, we will certainly make it." So gently. Not at all as if he were trying to talk himself into it, just how he saw it. He had an eye for goodness.

A little later he said, "Isn't it nice to see each ticket agent continuing to smile? They are really valiant people." I turned around and said: "Are you available for adoption?"

His easy positive energy, his upbeat attitude were so welcome. I come from a long line of Irish dreaders. People who think you are doing yourself a favor by expecting the worst so you won't be disappointed.

That young man was such a help to me. Usually what happens in situations like that in airports is that you get bombarded with people's negative energy. People swear and shake their fists and cover each other in rage and frustration and depression. For all of us standing in line near him, he turned us around in the other direction. I needed his help to overcome my dread.

In the end I was grateful the altimeter wasn't working. Even though I got to Boise ten hours later than I planned, I was able to receive his goodness, remember it, and share it.

16

Deepening Our Joy

Joy is the most infallible sign of the presence of God.

—Leon Bloy

On my list of valuable activities for dealing with chaos, keeping an eye out for goodness is followed immediately by the practice of deepening our joy. The energy of joy has great power for creation.

I began to think about the need to deepen joy during the period I have mentioned some years ago when my parents were both very ill, dying within a few months of each other. In those hard times it seemed more important than ever to open up to joy. In our family we definitely did not have any to waste.

I had begun to be aware of the importance of joy as a result of something my son Randy said one day. As background I want to describe Randy a little more for you.

Growing up, he was the original free spirit. There was no predicting what he might do or say, laughing, taking on the world. He was up for any adventure, and had a great sense of abiding luck. When he was in trouble he would get very charming.

Randy rushed headlong into life, and, as the result of one of the tidal waves of challenge generated by the energy of that rushing, he ended up in the Army in the Gulf War. The terrible things he experienced there changed him forever.

He came home with a kind of clarity, a pain-honed, certain, simple valuing of the life we are given. He expressed it sometimes with a religious overtone he had never used before, perhaps a style he had formed with other soldiers in the desert.

He came in from work one afternoon the summer after he got back and was talking to me about a person who was really getting on his nerves, an arrogant, insensitive person whom he had to deal with in his job. "He is *really* getting to me, Mom," he said in a furious tone. When Randy is angry he has a kind of fierce, glowering aura that takes up the whole room. Then he stopped himself and laughed: "I'm going to stop thinking about this," he said. "It's just the devil trying to steal my joy."

"What?"

"The devil. Trying to steal my joy."

I was stunned. That amazing sentence has stayed with me ever since. I have become more and more aware of times since then that I have felt the forces of the dark, which would be one translation of the devil; resentment and panic and broken hope, moving in to quell my joy. It has been a very useful awareness. I have learned from his example to try to guard against the theft.

Philosopher Leon Bloy said: "Joy is the most infallible sign of the presence of God." I love the wording of that. It explains to me why guarding it is so important. Why it would be exactly what the devil would try to steal. We need to protect the infallible sign of the presence of God from the enormous forces of disheartening—inside of us and outside of us.

Terrible things happen to us in our lives. Chaos comes. Broken bones and broken hearts, failure and angst, sometimes dreadful news in the middle of the night.

It is hard work not letting the dark overtake us. I remember as a little girl being afraid of the dark. All three of us sisters were. We slept in what we called the attic, what was really the top floor of a tall, narrow row house outside Georgetown in Washington, D.C.

Mom and Dad would leave the light on for us in the hall at the bottom of the stairs. Occasionally when they were walking down there by the door leading to the stairway they would inadvertently push the door shut. We would call out, "Don't close the door! Please don't close the door!" It was very important to us not to be up there in the dark.

Not staying in the dark is important for me now in a different way. I am trying to discover how to keep the light of joy shining up my stairs. How not to let the devil steal my joy.

Convinced of its importance, I work at opening more to joy. I try to savor moments of beauty, of laughter, of unexpected kindness. I try not to focus on everything I fear, on everything that bothers me, on all that could go wrong.

Of course, pain needs to be acknowledged and named, not ignored and repressed. We need to be with ourselves tenderly in our suffering. But it has been crucial in my life to try not to magnify pain's power. It has been essential to struggle against the takeover of dread and bitterness and rancor.

And to celebrate every time there's cause. "This is wallow time," Lona's step-sister, Peggy, said to me at the hospital after the lovely doctor almost danced in to tell us the news that there were no signs of cancer.

"Wallow time?" I asked, puzzled.

"It was an expression of my grandfather's," she explained. "He had a farm in the Tennessee mountains, raised a lot of pigs. That's where he got the expression. He taught me this: 'Life has hard times and good times. In the hard times, hang on. In the good times, wallow.' When you get news this good, it is pure and simple wallow time."

Wallow, celebrate, do things you look forward to with people you love. And pass it on. Pass on the joy.

I have been paying attention to how much it adds when I can share my happiness. I remember when Kadee's second baby was born. She was two weeks overdue, and they finally scheduled a C-section for December 18.

I was waiting in her hospital room in a rocking chair praying, almost holding my breath, trying not to think of all the possible complications in the particular history of this birth. There were many dangerous complexities connected to Kadee's health.

In only a few minutes I heard a cry that sounded like a newborn. "It couldn't be the baby already," I said to myself. "It must have been one of the infants in the nursery. "

But the crying grew closer and closer and Kadee's wonderful husband John, with the blue hospital scrubs worn over his clothes, came into the room alongside a nurse who turned out to be a grandmother herself. They showed me a beautiful dark-haired baby boy, naked and pink, umbilical cord clamped, tiny arms and legs thrashing as his voice continued to announce his determined entry into being. The nurse wrapped him up and put him in the basinette.

I walked over and touched his cheek. Tears welled up in my eyes. "John Andrew, you darling," I said, speaking aloud for the first time the name they had chosen. "I'm so glad you're here!"

I could feel the tension of closely guarded fears draining out of me. He was here. Safe. Peaceful now, eyes dark newborn blue, looking around. Long fingers and rounded toes curling and uncurling.

"Everything works," the nurse said grinning, "He wet all over the doctor and me right after delivery."

John moved over next to me and put his big finger in the middle of the baby's hand. The tiny fingers closed around it. "He's hanging on to me," he said, his voice husky with emotion. "He knows it's me." I turned aside to give them privacy. Big John and little John. Life from life.

A half-hour later I was in a grocery store, picking up some things Kadee had asked for. There were three people ahead of me in the checkout line. The young woman at the cash register asked the first person if, in the spirit of Christmas, they would want to add to their bill a little money with which the store would buy food for the poor. "Would you like to add five dollars?" she asked, "Or three? Or one?" The person was incensed: "What kind of gimmick is that? This damn bill is high enough already."

The checker was crestfallen and embarrassed. When she asked the next person she only mentioned adding three dollars or one. He grudgingly said, "Oh, all right, one." When the man in front of me stepped up, she did not mention it at all.

When it was my turn, I said "Wait a minute, didn't you say we could add money to our bill that the store would use to buy food at their wholesale rate and give it to people who need it for Christmas?"

"Yes," she said, "Would you like to give a dollar?"

"I heard you say one or three or five. Is that the limit? Why not twenty? Why not fifty? Why not more?"

She was plainly startled. "I guess so, if you want to," she said, smiling shyly.

"I *do* want to," I said. "My grandson was just born. Just now within the hour. John Andrew. Strong and whole and filled with promise. Find out about the limit. I want so much to share my joy."

Celebrate, wallow, share. Gather moments of joy. Relish them when they are happening, and remember them with flourishes.

We need to take note of songs, films, art, or plays that mediate joy in us and return to them, or keep them somehow to revisit. "Tie them up with a ribbon and save them in a box," as Oliver Twist sings of the beautiful morning in "Who Will Buy?"

My favorite image for the carefully gathered treasures is from Ray Bradbury's magnificent book *Dandelion Wine*, a book about a twelve-year-old boy named Douglas and summertime. He helped his grandfather make wine from the dandelions which grew in their yard surrounding the house with "the dazzle and glitter of molten sun."

He picked sacks of flowers, carrying them to the basement where Grandpa put them into the wine press, gently squeezing them. The liquid was then skimmed and bottled into clean catsup shakers and lined in sparkling rows in the cellar gloom.

Dandelion wine. The words were summer on the tongue. The wine was summer caught and stoppered . . . sealed away for opening on some January day with snow falling fast and the sun unseen for weeks or months. . . .

It is important to me to gather stories. It is like bottling the dandelion wine of joy to be decanted when the door at the bottom of the stairs is closed without a warning and the attic goes completely dark.

I especially prize the stories about narrow escapes, about great surprises, about against all odds, about in the nick of time.

One of my favorite nick of times happened when I had been giving a workshop at a retreat center in the midwest. I had a reservation on an 8:00 a.m. flight with three connections to California. It was the only flight that would make those connections to get me to San Diego in time for the keynote address I was scheduled to give that night.

I had called the airport limousine service twice, and they assured me the limo would come for me at 5:45 a.m. I had been warned that it was a long and congested drive to the airport and I needed to allow plenty of time. At 6:00, 6:15, 6:30, there was no sign of them. They did not answer their phone when I called to find out where they were.

At 7:00 a car pulled up in the front, but it was not the limo, it was one of the secretaries coming in early. I explained my plight, and, without hesitation, she said, "Throw your stuff in my car, we will make it!"

She pulled out into the choke of traffic with incredible skills, winding her way through trucks and vans and compact cars at about 55 mph. Wherever a gap opened up, she was through it. She glanced at me and laughed out loud. "You look worried, Pat," she said. "Don't be scared. I'm good at this—I always wanted to be a race car driver." We pulled up in front of the airport at 7:55.

She said, "You get your bag, I'll make sure they don't leave." She leapt through the door, glancing at the flight board, then sprinting through security. She didn't even bother waiting for her purse.

"Don't leave without her," she yelled to the stewardess about to close the door. "She deserves to make it. Besides, she's good company, you'll like her."

I came scrambling down the jetway with my bag and ticket and they let me on. I buckled up my seat belt, and looked out the window as we took off. She was standing on the hood of her car, waving to me. In the nick of time.

I heard an "against all odds" story from my mother the fall before she died. She was talking to me about when I was born during World War II. She was describing it for the first time from the perspective of her parents. I think they were on her mind a lot because she knew she was close to joining them.

She told me that my father was a captain in the infantry when the war began. When he was ordered to a war assignment she took my older sister and went to her parents' home in New Jersey where she had grown up. A few months later I was born. We lived in what we called "the little house" which had been my grandfather's law office across the corner lot from the "big house" where my grandparents lived. We stayed there for four years.

As she was recalling those times, I realized that I had very clear memories of them myself. I could visualize the pattern of light the venetian blinds made in the room where I was put to take my nap. I could remember the startling purple-blue of morning glories on the fence in Grandpa's garden in the yard, and how when he first saw us each day he would greet us always by saying, "Good morning, Glory."

For a long time I had known that it was a good thing for us to be in our little house with Grandpa and Grandma in the big house, but not until Mom began to talk about it that fall did I know what a good thing it had been for them. I had never realized that while we were there Grandma was diagnosed with cancer. I vaguely knew that she had died of cancer, but I never understood the timing.

"What a desolate time it would have been for them without us there," Mom said to me as she was telling the story. She described the terrible fear for the whole world at war. Her parents had particular anguish because their only son and both their West Point sons-in-law were overseas in danger. And on top of that, Grandma was facing long, relentless suffering and death, and Grandpa was facing the loss of her, the great and tender love of his entire life.

Into the midst of all that fear and death we came. And suddenly their lives were taken up with the incessant demands of little ones. In counterpoint to the horror and tragedy as the list of killed or missing grew at the town hall, there was the dramatic progress of tiny lives. A first tooth. A first step. The first sounds like "Grandpa" or "Grandma." First days out of diapers.

Time that would have been endless with worry and suffering was filled with life. Tea parties with acorn caps under huge oak trees in the fall. Helium balloons, sparklers and flags on the Fourth of July as the parade came right by the house on Main Street. Stories read aloud and dolls to dress and simple card games. Grandpa raked huge piles of red and yellow leaves for us to jump into, and later helped us roll great balls of snow for snow families with carrot noses. Grandma taught us the alphabet and numbers and about important things like guardian angels and St. Patrick and the snakes.

The war ended. All our family men survived, but Grandma died soon after.

"As strange as it seems," Mom said reflecting on the story when I was with her, "those were really happy years. Hard years, but years with lots of joy. If there had not been a war, your father and I would have been stationed somewhere far away. Kansas, maybe, or the Philippines. They would have missed the days when you were small. My mother's final days would have been so bleak. Against all odds, they were filled with life."

Against all odds, in the nick of time, narrow escape.

I will end the chapter with a tale I love of narrow escape. It happened with my Dad when he was eighty-nine with Alzheimer's disease advancing relentlessly. This was the period after Mom could no longer care for him and he was living with a remarkable family, the Chambers, who for many years have kept Alzheimer's patients in their home.

It was after he had been there for a while that the people of the town finished building a monument to the men in their area who had lost their lives in Vietnam. There were quite a few of them for such a small town. Somehow it was arranged that General William Westmoreland himself, who had been Commander-in-Chief in Vietnam, would come and dedicate the monument.

I have mentioned that Dad was in the Army for a career, and when Judy, the mother of the family and the main care-giver of Dad, saw an article in the paper she asked Dad if he knew General Westmoreland. It was one of his clearer days, and his long term memory was often quite good. "Westy! Why sure," he said. "He was behind me at West Point, but we were stationed together. We are friends."

So she told him Westmoreland was coming and asked if he wanted to go. He not only wanted to go, he wanted to wear his uniform in Westmoreland's honor. And so he did.

When Westmoreland arrived and took the stage, he looked out at the audience as he began his remarks. Right away he spotted Dad. "George! Hello! So glad to see you!" he said, and then launched into his dedication speech.

When he finished and completed the ceremony, he left the stage and came right over to where Dad was sitting. "George, you look great! I just wish I could stay and catch up with you, hear what you're doing these days. There is a helicopter waiting. I have to move right on, I'm sorry. I really appreciate your coming out. It means the world to me. I have always admired you."

"Thank you," Dad said, smiling, shaking his hand.

The whole town watched as Westmoreland climbed into the helicopter. They kept watching as Judy proudly led Dad to the car. Buckling up the seat belt with tears in his eyes, Dad said, "What am I getting all choked up about?" He had already begun to forget.

It was a narrow escape, but he pulled it off. Sixty seconds, two minutes, that's about all his brain could do before the tangled neurons mixed the signals. Westmoreland never knew there was anything wrong. He took Dad's presence for the honor it truly was.

There is radical goodness in life. Telling the stories keeps the devil from stealing the joy.

17

Hanging in There

It ain't over 'til it's over.

—Yogi Berra

I have been listing things that help me deal with chaos, things for the times of the knotted stomach, treasures for the moments when dread is moving in fast: believing and doing, reaching out and noticing, receiving and remembering, connecting with life.

There's something else that helps. It is a reminder to myself: "Hang in there 'til the end. There is no telling what could happen." One of my favorite things to say out loud—someday perhaps I'll hang it up in needlepoint—is Yogi Berra's saying: "It ain't over 'til it's over."

I was amazed to discover the end of the story of Job. I don't know how I had missed it all these years. I had only thought of the Book of Job as a tale of endless suffering. Once, late at night, I was poring over the small print of my Jerusalem Bible when I discovered something that stunned me: an Epilogue (Job 42:10-17) in which:

*Yahweh restored Job's fortunes. . . . More than
that, Yahweh gave him double what he had
before. And all his brothers and all his sisters and*

*all his friends of former times came to see him
and sat down at table with him. They showed
him every sympathy, and comforted him for all
the evils Yahweh had inflicted on him. . . . He
came to own fourteen thousand sheep, six
thousand camels, a thousand yoke of oxen and a
thousand she-donkeys. He had seven sons and
three daughters" [same as before]. Throughout
the land there were no women as beautiful as the
daughters of Job.* And their father gave them
inheritance rights like their brothers *[emphasis
added].*

*After his trials, Job lived on until he was a
hundred and forty years old, and saw his children
and his children's children up to the fourth
generation. Then Job died, an old man and full
of days.*

An astounding ending! Job, the symbol of one who suffers
innocently, has everything returned to him and more.

I pondered for a long time the special detail of Job's daughters. Women were rarely mentioned in those ancient writings.
Daughters had no inheritance rights at all. It is as if Job, when
he has been through his experience of suffering and loss, sees
the beauty of the ones who legally had nothing. To the ones to
whom nothing was owed, a rich inheritance was given.

Job's largesse seemed to me to be an echo of Yahweh whose
gifts are not lost or earned by right. They come from Mystery,
the depth of whose loving purpose we cannot comprehend. The
end of the story of Job is like the end of other stories I con-
sciously bring to mind when I feel trapped in deep worry. I try
to think of things like Mr. Boney or like Polly and Ben.

About five miles outside the town where I raised my kids,
a man named Everett Boney lives. Mr. Boney has worked with
cows all his life long, and is still doing it in his late 70s. When

he was eighteen he was kicked in the eye by a horse and from then on was blind in that eye.

Sometime before the story was told to me, cataracts had begun to grow over his good eye. He went to an eye doctor, but the doctor said he wouldn't take the chance of operating on it because it was the only good eye. Mr. Boney was really discouraged, thinking he would gradually lose all his sight.

Someone suggested he seek a second opinion, so Mr. Boney drove a hundred miles to Tampa to see a specialist. That doctor looked at his eye with the cataracts and said, "I think I can fix that." He operated on it, and was completely successful. Mr. Boney's one eye could see perfectly.

Then the doctor said, "What's the matter with your other eye?" Mr. Boney said, "Oh, it's useless. I was kicked in the eye by a horse when I was eighteen and it's been blind ever since."

The doctor said, "I think I can fix that." He operated on the other eye, and completely restored the sight. Mr. Boney at nearly eighty now sees better than he has since he was eighteen.

That story is good for me when I need help to hang in there, to keep from foreclosing on hope. So does the story of my neighbor for many years whom I'll call Polly. She and her husband, Ben, were about seventy when they moved across the street. They had no children of their own, and they kind of adopted me. They had both been in World War II, she as an Army nurse, he as a combat soldier. It was interesting to me how that war experience remained for them the most significant period of their lives.

They both worked hard, keeping the house and yard spotless, but they argued all the time—morning, noon, and night. It was almost as if World War II still raged behind their walls. They really couldn't stand each other, but they couldn't divorce because they didn't have enough money to live separately.

They were both extremely kind to me, helping me with the little things and the major ones. Once my house flooded when I was away and they discovered it and dealt with the mess. I think working on that project was a little truce for them. But soon they went back to fighting. It was hard for me to be at their house because they would each interrupt the other one to tell their side of it, wanting me to say who was right.

Well, after about ten years, Polly had a stroke paralyzing her on one side. She was sent to a rehab hospital about an hour-and-a-half away.

Ben went there every day, all day—he only came home to sleep and change. Then he drove back to the hospital, working with her in the physical therapy exercise room hour after hour, day after day. With his help she learned to walk again and went home.

About eight weeks after that Ben died. Some time later Polly moved to an assisted living facility where I used to visit her. Most of the time she just sat out in the common room. She wasn't interested in doing crafts or going on field trips. She just sat.

"What do you think about when you sit here, Polly?" I asked her.

She smiled. "I think about falling in love."

"You mean long ago in Brooklyn?"

"Oh no, dear. In the rehab hospital. I fell in love with Ben and he fell in love with me. I just sit here and think about that. What a miracle. If that hadn't happened I would be sitting here bitter. Dried up. Hating. Still at war. Now I sit here grateful. We loved each other! At the end, we fell in love. And, maybe I shouldn't say this, but it's true: it might be better that he didn't live too long. I'm not sure if we could have kept it up! I am just so glad it lasted long enough. I never get tired of thinking about it. I sit here saying to myself: 'Imagine that! We fell in love.'"

I hugged her, and there were tears on both our faces.

We don't know the ending 'til the ending. Don't give up, I say inside, retelling these dear stories. Trust. Which does not mean a miracle for every outcome. I always need to quickly say that. Of course, a lot of bad things happen. But somehow Love will be there. I look back on life and see the truth of that, look back on years of migraines, look back at when my first son at full term was stillborn, look back at heartbreak, bitter disappointment. Still, Love was always with me. Love hangs in there.

I have a new belief about endurance. It is a fragile conviction, but it is passionately held. What I am starting to believe is this: If you push all the way through the pain, on the other side of it is laughter. Here is the story that gave me the beginning of this belief:

It was the summer of my fiftieth birthday, a summer I have mentioned as a time of great turmoil in our family. It was a year of prolonged exhaustion, merciless endings, shocking diagnoses, and shattered peace.

I had long planned to give myself a retreat for this birthday. I had a series of ideas, but one after another they had fallen through. Finally I had a great inspiration. A woman from California came to Notre Dame where I was living to give a workshop on yoga and massage. I was free to go to some of it and was even able to sign up for a half hour of massage. I asked her if she ever did massage retreats. To focus on my body seemed like a great gift to give it for the fiftieth anniversary of its birth!

She said she often did that kind of retreat for people and would be glad to do it with me. We agreed on dates. I bought my airline ticket.

About three weeks before I was due to go I called her to get the final details. There was a tense silence on the line when I mentioned my arrival date. She had written it down in a different month. She had taken other commitments on the road for most of the time I would be coming. She felt awful about it, and since I had a non-refundable ticket, she said I could stay in one of the buildings of their center. She would leave books and art supplies and food, even her car for me to use. She would be back the last day I would be there.

I was very disappointed, but I really wanted to make a retreat, so I accepted. I was all alone in the house, a house that had been built to hold about twenty people. My small sounds echoed in the polished hallways. I got very jumpy. There were strange noises in the plumbing. The phone would ring, but no one would be on the line.

In the middle of the first night I heard truck sounds very close, and then the breaking of glass and the scraping of metal. I couldn't imagine what it was. I lay there telling myself I was dumb to be frightened. Then I remembered reading stories about burglaries where the thieves backed a semi-truck up to a house and just loaded everything onto it.

"I can't just lie here and let someone rip off everything these nuns have," I told myself. So I made myself get up and investigate. What I discovered was that just across the narrow street was a warehouse. It must have had a nightshift. The trucks drove in from a factory somewhere and dumped glass and metal into huge bins with the scraping, crashing sound that had startled me from sleep. There was no danger, but they were the night sounds every night.

The days were hard. All the things that worried me surrounded me. I did everything I knew to do. I read, I used the art supplies, I listened to the music. I tried to cook. She had left me groceries, very healthy things. . . . I know that when you are worried, the best thing you could do for yourself is to eat all health food. I know that. But I couldn't warm up to all the kinds of beans. The brown rice did nothing for my angst.

So I got out of there. I asked for corner tables in expensive restaurants and ordered all the decadent desserts. I went to public gardens. I walked along the water.

In the day I wished that it were time to sleep, and in the night I longed for light to come again. It was as if I could hear the harsh breathing of "the ogre." The ogre has long been my metaphor for the worst that stalks me: the fears that wait beside my bed and pounce when there are any interludes of rest.

Finally it was my last day and she came home. She was lovely and welcoming, but I was so ragged from the pain, I could hardly even be polite. There is a kind of anger I have noticed that can build up in me in times of chaos. When other people are very upbeat and hopeful it can have the effect of

increasing my sense of isolation, because I have no correspon-
ding quickening of consolation or hope. Their trying to point
out the meaningfulness of my experience is distancing because
it doesn't feel meaningful to me and I cannot seem to find the
part of me that once found meaning. It was that sort of anger
I felt toward her, and then I felt thoroughly ashamed because
she was being extremely gracious and sympathetic.

After a while she took me to the massage room and began
to work on the layered tension in my neck and back.
Somewhere in the midst of it, I began to cry. Then waves and
waves of sadness, fear, and pain spasmed in a kind of primal
sobbing.

She said "Pat, sometimes this happens. All the unspeakable
things cry out to be released. Let go. Let go, little one, let go. It
is your pain, and it is the sorrow of the world. Let go."

When I left her I went to my room and slept for fifteen
hours. The next day I felt better, and I was going to see her
once more before I got on my plane at noon. I was a little wary
when I saw her for our session, reluctant to start the tears again.
I suggested maybe I'd just learn a few yoga stretches. Nothing
with emotional content.

She thought more massage would be a good idea. I tried to
just let go. OK, if I sobbed again, I did. I would just see what
happened, not try to figure it all out.

What happened was completely unexpected. She was
working on some muscles in my calves. She had soothing
music on and incense burning. She talked to me in her beautiful voice that sounded like it could heal the whole world. She
said something meant to be reassuring like, "There is room for
all your pain in the universe," or "There are all the resources
you need for healing in the universe." I can't remember any
more just what it was. What I remember is that it struck me
funny. The incongruity of it. The saying was just so orderly, and
my life was such a mess.

At first I just smiled thinking how far my life was from the
concept of an orderly universe. Then I started to laugh.

Disorderly lines started popping into my head. They were lines from a book my son Boo had read aloud on a family trip we took in June. He likes to bring books for us to take turns reading. It was a book of quotations, a collection of outrageous things famous people had said. A lot of it was pretty earthy. I just started saying them out loud.

Erma Bombeck saying: "The only reason I would take up jogging is to hear heavy breathing again."

Mae West saying: "I only like two kinds of men, domestic and foreign."

Miss Piggy saying: "Only eat what you can lift."

The Raymond Chandler line: "It was a blonde; a blonde to make a Bishop kick a hole in a stained glass window."

I laughed and laughed. She laughed too. But she looked worried. She asked me to close my eyes. "What do you see?" she asked.

I closed my eyes. (I have no idea how these things work.) I looked . . . "I see a clearing in a forest," I said.

She told me to look and see if there was anything with me in the clearing.

I looked again. Sitting there across the clearing was a great Buddha! A giant Buddha. As big as the Buddha in Beppu, Japan I had seen as a little girl. The Buddha was laughing. He was absolutely cracked-up laughing. His beautiful, kind face was crinkled with merriment and his wonderful belly shook like the bowl full of jelly in the Christmas rhyme about Santa. His three chins, his rolls of fat, all shook with laughter. That's when I knew: *being thin is highly overrated.*

Buddha. The Enlightened One. What does enlightenment mean? Maybe it's this: If you push all the way through the pain, on the other side of it is laughter. When you laugh, the ogre's grip is loosened. The adversary, which is what the word Satan means, is turned back. Today at least, the devil will not steal your joy.

Two thousand years ago, early in the morning, on the first day of the week, two women shattered and broken-hearted made their way to a tomb in a hillside outside Jerusalem. They were prepared to anoint the mutilated body of their beloved one, Jesus of Nazareth, who had been crucified.

When they got there the stone in front of the tomb had been rolled back, the gravecloths laid aside, and the body of their beloved one was not there. An angel said to them: "Why do you seek the Living One among the dead?"

John Shea suggests that if we could have heard the sound of the resurrection, it would have been the sound of laughter.

It ain't over 'til it's over.

18

Praying

*At its best, prayer is not a way of being pious but
a creative way of being human.*

—John Shea

The final thing that I will mention that helps to deal with chaos
is prayer. It is really woven in some way through all the other
things I've mentioned, since prayer is not so much words as living in the presence of God.

For me, however, in order to do that kind of living I need
some specific prayer time. I have had many prayer styles in my
life, often wondering if I were doing it "right." I now think perhaps the most important aspect is that I pray in some way that
appeals to me. I want it to be something I look forward to, not
something I force upon myself. Both ancient mystics and current theologians have said that the purpose of prayer is not to
do a lot of talking, but to experience God's deep and personal
love for us. That is much easier for me if I feel at home with
how I pray.

I like to pray looking out my window. God's presence in
the beauty of the world is very real to me. I like to pray early
with tea or coffee, in a lovely cup I've used a long time; or late,
with warm milk, looking at the stars. I like to pray with quiet
music. I like to pray with those I love.

There is a book of daily readings called *The Daybook* by Marv and Nancy Hiles from the Iona Center that I enjoy so much I have to discipline myself not to read the whole week at one time, but wait until each day comes. My husband and I take turns reading it aloud.

Another rich form of prayer for me is the silent, holy space of meditation.

It means a lot to me to pray with scripture. I have started writing passages in one of those beautiful blank books so I can find them when I want them. I go back to them again and again.

Some that speak to me in chaos are these:

Yahweh is my light and my salvation,
*   whom need I fear?*
Yahweh is the fortress of my life,
*   of whom should I be afraid?*
*   —Psalm 27*

***

If I flew to the point of sunrise,
or westward across the sea,
Your hand would still be guiding me,
your right hand holding me.

If I asked darkness to cover me,
and light to become night around me,
that darkness would not be dark to you,
night would be as light as day.
*   —Psalm 139*

***

Do not be afraid, for I have redeemed you;
I have called you by your name, you are mine. . . .
You are precious in my eyes . . .
you are honored and I love you.
*   —Isaiah 43:2, 4*

***

In the world you will have trouble,
but be brave:
I have conquered the world.
      —John 16:33

***

Do not worry about tomorrow: tomorrow will take care of itself.
Each day has enough trouble of its own.
      —Matthew 6:34

***

I am certain of this: neither death nor life, no angel, no prince,
nothing that exists, nothing still to come, not any power, or
height or depth, nor any created thing, can ever come between
us and the love of God made visible in Christ Jesus Our Lord.
      —Romans 8:38-39

I put hymns in my book too, when they appeal to me. I love the old Shaker song, "How Can I Keep From Singing?" and wrote its lines:

What storm can shake this inmost calm,
while to this rock I'm clinging?
If love is Lord of heaven and earth,
how can I keep from singing?

Whenever I pray I always think of how lucky I am to have the luxury of this time. With all the new babies in our family I am very aware of how parents of young children have almost no time at all to themselves. I remember well when my only really private prayer time was in the bathtub. Even then someone was usually calling me under the door! I always think of young parents, or people holding down two jobs, or people caring for someone full time, when I have this quiet time. I know the time to center myself in the goodness of God is a gift of sheer goodness in itself.

There is one prayer I've come to think as the sum of all the others and the central prayer in chaos.

Ironically, I learned this from my mother. I smile just thinking about it because she was an improbable source for theological summaries. She was not much interested in theology as a subject. She was not much for long talks, or even short talks, on meaning. She was more for practical discussions, for learning useful things that would make life simpler or easier. She was interested in facts: where people had lived, what they had done, how many children they had had.

Something else that interested her was words. One of her great remedies for pain was doing crossword puzzles. "They are better than those medicines that fog your mind and make your stomach queasy."

More into words than meaning, more into the bottom line than theological speculation, that was Mom. If there was an accident, something spilled or burning on the stove, some kind of homey crisis, she would roll her eyes and say "Well, Pat, I guess you're going to find some *meaning* in this . . . let's just clean it up."

She was puzzled at the response people had to my first book, *Lessons of the Heart*. I used to send her some of the letters people wrote to me, and she would say, amazed: "Boy, the people your book takes on, it really takes on." Her favorite part was that the book earned me money when I wasn't doing any more work. She thought I worked too hard.

All this is to say that you would go to Mom to have a hem pinned or an up-to-date analysis of the evening news more than you would go for an uplifting sentiment or a sustaining theological thought. She would often say, "I am not sentimental or pious," as if she had been graciously delivered of some intolerable burden. Her faith was very strong, but it was entirely matter-of-fact.

In her final hospitalization my sisters and I were gathered around her bed feeling the helplessness that overcomes you when someone you love very much is suffering. We decided to say the rosary. She had been lying very still with her eyes closed, appearing deeply asleep. We got through the prayers on about the first three beads when she opened her eyes and glared straight at us: "Really, girls," she said, "I'm *not* the type!" We grinned at each other and put the rosaries away.

And so, because words about meaning or reflections on God were very few and far between for Mom, it is surprising that it was Mom who emphasized for me the prayer I now think of as the central prayer during chaos. (She would like it that it is the ultimate punch line. "Even though it's not a joke," she might say, "for once I got the punch line right.")

The prayer came out of something that happened in the Holy Week of her last year when she was too weak to go to church. I was on spring break and staying with her in her apartment. I had gone to the Good Friday service with my sister Peggy at her parish. Every year they offer the Seven Last Words service and ask seven lay members of the parish to do reflections on the words the gospels give as the last words of Jesus. I was telling Mom later that the pastor had asked Peggy to participate, and that her meditation was on Jesus' saying: "Into your hands I commend my spirit."

"Oh," said Mom, "I think that is the most important one. That is what it is about, all our lives long, and especially at the end. I just hope I am lucid enough at the end to remember to say that when I am dying. I'd really like to say that when I die."

She was silent for a while. This had been so much not her usual conversation that she looked as if she were feeling a little embarrassed. Then she took a deep breath and continued:

"If I am not conscious, or if I am somehow too distracted, I hope one of you girls will say it for me: 'Into your hands I commend my spirit.'"

The afternoon of Mom's death Peggy was there. Peggy who had been so faithful for so long, both strong and tender with her care. Mom was not conscious at the end, and Peggy did remember. With Mom's hands in hers she said the words for her: "Into your hands I commend my Spirit."

If she were here now Mom would say, "There you have the punch line for us all. That's it. Put yourself into the hands of God."

19

The Ending: Amen

This is the last day of writing this book. I need to finish it and mail it to the publisher by Monday.

With the exquisite parallelism that life sometimes offers, today is the last day before my new grandchild is born. Boo and Caroline and Hunter, who is almost three, have been waiting for the baby any day for several weeks. The doctor told Caroline Monday that if it had not come before today he would induce her labor. They were to go to the hospital at 5:30 this morning. I have been up praying, sipping coffee, watching the sky get light.

I keep remembering when I was in Caroline's place, the apprehension and excitement, the pains taking your breath and blotting out all other awareness, and then the ebbs that let the magnitude of the moment surface: It is *now*, the culmination of all these complex months of pregnancy, of all the years of two lives on the way to making this new one.

I remember so clearly when Boo was born, three-and-a-half weeks overdue. In those days they rarely induced you. My phone had never stopped ringing: Haven't you had that baby *yet*?

We were out on a lovely walk in the late Arizona afternoon, Kadee and Randy throwing pebbles in a small, slow stream, when my labor started. I fed everyone dinner when we got home, pork chops and rice and fresh green beans. I knew not to eat anything myself. After I did the dishes and made sure the bathrooms were relatively clean we called the friends who were going to stay with the children while we went to the hospital.

It was always the smell of the hospital: disinfectant perhaps, floor wax, alcohol that really brought it home to me. And the purposeful stride of nurses and doctors. The paging on the intercom. The urgency. Now. This is it. The curtain's going up, no turning back. "OK, kid, you're leaving the wings. You're about to be on."

And now Boo is there with Caroline, the curtain going up on this little life. There is great curiosity throughout the family: on both sides all the grandchildren have been boys, a total of eight. Will this one be a girl?

Little one, whoever you are, you are so welcome.

Dear God, let them feel your love surrounding them.

It is six hours since I put that prayer on paper. My concern is growing. It's after two o'clock and the doctor told Caroline the baby would be born by noon. Perhaps he was being glib. She had a such a long labor last time, he might have been wanting to put her at ease.

I try not to think about the problem with her heart that made her have open heart surgery when she was thirteen. I try not to think of stories I have heard about babies, or my own Joseph stillborn. "Into your hands . . . into your hands. . . ."

It has been storming off and on all day, beginning before light. That is unusual in Florida in summer. There are mostly big brash storms each afternoon that start and stop in no time. This storm slacks a bit but then returns. I keep turning off my computer to protect it when the lightning comes in close. Then I walk around. Make tea. I've cleaned out the refrigerator and weeded out the sock drawers. Next I'll do the wrapping paper box.

I keep going back to prayer, and also know this whole long day of vigil is a prayer. I pray for all the mothers in the world, in labor, giving birth today. I pray for all our mothers. . . .

Something splendid happened about an hour ago. I was sitting in the bedroom, eyes closed, praying, when I was jolted to standing upright by a monstrous flash of lightning and such a crack of thunder that dogs throughout the neighborhood were barking and car alarms went off.

I ran to the window, looking out across the water, shocked with the nearness of the danger. "I don't like this as a symbol," I said loudly. Then I thought of Max and rattlesnakes and peacocks. I struggled to remember goodness.

At that moment—I wouldn't blame you if you think I made this up, but honestly, it happened—I saw a dolphin in the water! My favorite sign of hope. The fin, and then the back, curving in the gray light, hardly splashing. It stayed there, up and under, up and under, moving in a circle, until the rain came down so hard I couldn't see the water anymore.

In this day so steeped in Mystery the message came again: "I am with you, I am with you, I am with you."

The phone just rang which I grabbed in a split second. "Good afternoon, I have a wonderful offer for you . . . no money down . . . low interest rate. . . ." A telemarketer.

I think I'll scrub the kitchen floor.

And then another ring: A GIRL! A GIRL! Hannah Elizabeth Livingston. Nine pounds, five ounces. WOW!!

"She is a darlin'," Boo said softly. "She is looking at me now. I've been with them all the time. It all went really smoothly. Caroline was . . . *great.* " Relief and pride, great gladness in his voice.

"When was she born?"

"At 1:06," he said.

The tears of joy that started when I heard her name ran down my face. That was the moment of the dolphin in the bay. Of course! I guess the lightning was her cue to come on stage. Oh little girl-child, how glad I am that you are in my play!

Well. What a day to do the final chapter of my book about creation.

***

There have been many pages, many chapters since this book began. A lot has happened in my life and, I'm sure, in your life as we have looked together at the interweavings of struggle and strengthening, difficulty and deliverance. These threads overlap and intertwine, echo and repeat, intersect and double back. All of it forms a pattern, like the beautiful, intricate geometric fractals of science and nature, the pattern of the love and the pain, the fear and the trust, the snakes and the flowers.

So many good things happen. But sooner or later, in some form or other, as my friend Benni would say, there is a kink in the ointment.

Mystery grapples with us from the time we make our first appearance until we ask those who love us to pray for us as we die.

Along the way there are dolphins and head lice, red plaid dresses and great black Labradors that sit beside our feet. We learn to live with mess and try not to let the devil steal our joy. We might wear a curler to a White House dinner or cause the collapse of a barn. Through it all we journey to compassion as we are, again and again, broken open and poured out. We hang on and we wallow, pushing through pain into laughter, because, riding out the *tohu wa bohu*, we discover that we are all in this together.

I began by saying this was a book about struggle. I said it would mostly be stories and they would all point to the same thing. Life is filled with struggle. Struggle is filled with Love.

A final story.

It is a story I'm convinced that Mom had a part in. It has been fascinating to see that she has kept on influencing our lives even after she is "sitting on God's right hand."

When Mom died, I had been divorced for twenty years. For fifteen years I had had an annulment from the Catholic church. I really went through the annulment process to please her because she worried a great deal about my being alone. We had a lot of conversations about it. I'd tell her that I thought there were much worse things than being alone, like feeling alone even when you are not.

She would say she wasn't worried about me now, when I was strong and had things I really liked to do, which, though they didn't pay that well, still paid enough to live on if I was careful and the kids pulled their weight. She was worried about when I was old and sick, like she had been for a long time.

So we had a lot of conversations, and I finally went through the annulment process. I had some wonderful relationships with men through the years, deep, loving friendships. But marriage did not seem to be the right direction for any of them.

My friend Gene Lauer said to me one day, "Pat, what do you think are the chances you will ever marry again?" It was in April of the year after my parents died.

"Less than one percent," I replied. "I never really think about it anymore."

A couple of weeks later it was Mother's Day, May 8. The first Mother's Day after Mom's death. I woke up thinking about her and missing her a lot, wondering how I could best spend the day doing things in her memory.

I first decided I would clean my closets (one of her most characteristic pastimes) and maybe even turn my mattress. (I couldn't remember the last time I had turned it.) Then I thought: "I'll eat chocolate!" Chocolate was her idea of the only worthwhile food group.

As I was planning these activities, the phone rang. It startled me, because she and I had talked every Sunday for the last thirty years.

When I answered the phone a man said "Pat, this is a voice out of your past, from twenty-five years ago. This is Howard Gordon. I have never forgotten you during that time, and I have often wondered how you were. I have just managed to track you down. Do you have a few minutes to talk?"

I was trying to place him when he said: "I still have red hair."

Then I remembered clearly: Of course! Howard. Bright and appreciative, very much alive. My first husband was his commanding officer in the Army legal corps. He and his wife had been stationed with us in Texas, and we had done a lot of things with them. Their marriage, he told me, had ended fifteen years ago. I told him mine had been over for twenty.

We talked for half an hour, first swapping stories, then cutting through small talk to what life meant to us, what we found worthwhile. "What gives you joy?" we asked. "What gives you peace?" It was an extraordinary conversation.

I had been getting ready for church, so I brought the talk to a close, thanking him for calling, for taking the trouble to look me up, for wishing me well after all those years. I drove to church smiling. "Mom, if this isn't just like you!" I called up to heaven, "Sending me a gentleman caller." That phrase from *The Glass Menagerie* was one she used. "Have you had any gentlemen callers?" she would ask.

A few days later he called again. Then he flew fifteen hundred miles to take me to dinner. He arrived carrying a beautifully wrapped package that turned about to be the exact kind of chocolates I always brought my mother. A very obscure kind. When she was in the hospital, close to dying, eating nothing the hospital gave her on the trays, I would come with those chocolates, and she would eat every one. When he gave me the box and I untied the rose ribbon and saw what they were, I was stunned. I could almost hear Mom's chuckle.

I said nothing about it to him at the time. We saw quite a bit of each other that summer when I went home for the break between semesters to the town where I raised my children. His Tampa law firm was not too far away. One evening at dinner I brought up the chocolates.

"Now that's the strangest thing," he said. "I never give people candy—especially people I don't know. You don't know whether they ever eat candy. Like I wouldn't bring wine to someone if I didn't know if they ever drank. I might bring a book, or flowers, not candy. But there I was on my way to see you, changing planes in the O'Hare airport in Chicago, and suddenly I found myself in some candy store paying for that box of chocolates! I couldn't explain it to you."

"I could explain it to you," I said to myself, perfectly picturing Mom grabbing him by the back of his suit jacket and dragging him into the candy shop. "Pat is going to need a lot of help for this to get through to her."

He had brought the chocolates in May. The conversation about the candy was in July. He and I got engaged in October. The following June in the chapel of our program I married him wearing my mother's mother's dress.

The wedding was glorious. People still talk about it. The gathering of friends and family who were delighted at our happiness took part with so much love in the ceremony we designed, in the simple reception of such festivity.

I tell this story not meaning to imply that marriage is the "happily ever after." Anyone who has been married knows it is a very worthwhile but challenging institution.

I tell it because it is a kind of paradigm of all our lives. It is an enfleshment of the Good News. Pain does not have the final say. It ain't over 'til it's over. The darkness does not, in the end, overcome the light.

In this world or the next, somehow, somewhere, against all odds, life is stronger than death. The mess is blessed. Love wins. Creation comes from chaos once again.

Amen.

Resources

Chapter 2. James Gleick, *Chaos: Making A New Science* (New York: Penguin Books 1987), p. 94.

Chapter 4. Roy Shoffner, monument guide book *Pest of Honor*, 1988.

Chapter 5. Michael Himes, *Doing the Truth in Love* (Mahwah, NJ: Paulist Press 1995), p. 62.

Chapter 8. Joseph Bernadin, *The Gift of Peace* (New York: Bantam, Doubleday, Dell Publishing, 1998).

Chapter 10. C. S. Lewis, *The Lion, The Witch and The Wardrobe* (New York: Collier Books, 1970), p. 103.

Chapter 12. "February: Thinking of Flowers" in *Otherwise-New and Selected Poems*, Jane Kenyon (St. Paul, MN: Graywolf Press, 1996).

Chapter 13. A. A. Milne, *Winnie-the-Pooh* (New York: Puffin Books, 1992), p. 30.

A. A. Milne, *The House at Pooh Corner* (New York: Puffin Books, 1992), pp. 132-133.

Chapter 15. Demetrius Dumm, OSB, *Cherish Christ Above All* (Mahwah, NJ: Paulist Press, 1996), p. 77.

Chapter 16. Ray Bradbury, *Dandelion Wine* (New York: Bantam Books, 1976), p. 12.

Chapter 18. John Shea, *The God Who Fell From Heaven* (Niles, IL: Argus Communications, 1979), p. 20.

A sought-after public speaker, **Patricia Livingston** inspires audiences with down-to-earth tales of everyday living. "People identify with my stories because I speak of ordinary, imperfect life. They connect with me because they realize that my life and their lives are similar—we meet in shared human experience." Besides leading workshops, retreats, and seminars throughout the United States and abroad, Livingston is an award-winning writer whose work

has been featured in *Praying, St. Anthony Messenger, Studies in Formative Spirituality*, and *U.S. Catholic*. In 1990, Livingston was awarded the U.S. Catholic Award for furthering the cause of women in the Catholic Church. Her previous book, *Lessons of the Heart*, with over 30,000 copies sold, provides encouragement in the face of life's hectic, stress-filled demands. Livingston lives with her husband, Howard Gordon, in Tampa, Florida.

Through every moment of this day: Be w/ me
  " " day of all this week; "
  " " week of all this year: "   "
  " " year of all this life: "   "
So that when time is past,
By grace I may at last,
Be w/ you Lord
God be in my head, + in my understand
  " mine eyes;   looking
  my mouth,   speaking

On the Bus with Rosa Parks